Sunny Skies From the Valley

Behind Growing Faith, A Debilitating Disease

SHARON ANA ENTRESS

All proceeds the author receives from the sale of this book will be donated to the St. John's Foundation in Rochester, New York, the Upstate New York Chapter of the ALS Association and Christian ministries.

Sunny Skies From the Valley
Behind Growing Faith, A Debilitating Disease
Copyright © 2016 by Sharon Ana Entress.
All rights reserved. No part of this book may be reproduced in any form without written permission from the author.

Cover art and design and photography on divider pages by Gerald E. Lange. Copyright © 2016. www.geraldlange.com Family photo taken by Patricia McDonald.

Some names used in this book have been changed at the request of the person involved.

Scriptures taken from the Holy Bible, New International Version®, NIV®. Copyright © 1973, 1978, 1984, 2011 by Biblica, Inc.™ Used by permission of Zondervan. All rights reserved worldwide. www.zondervan.com The "NIV" and "New International Version" are trademarks registered in the United States Patent and Trademark Office by Biblica, Inc.™

Scripture quotations marked (NIrV) are taken from the Holy Bible, New International Reader's Version®, NIrV® Copyright © 1995, 1996, 1998, 2014 by Biblica, Inc.™ Used by permission of Zondervan. All rights reserved worldwide. www.zondervan.com The "NIrV" and "New International Reader's Version" are trademarks registered in the United States Patent and Trademark Office by Biblica, Inc.™

Some content taken from BEAUTIFUL BATTELFIELDS, by Bonita Stern. Copyright © 2013. Used by permission of NavPress. All rights reserved. Represented by Tyndale House Publishers, Inc.

ISBN-13: 978-1535331685
ISBN-10: 1535331682

*I know God won't give me anything I can't handle.
I just wish he didn't trust me so much.*

MOTHER TERESA

ACKNOWLEDGEMENTS

If anyone told me a few years ago that my mother would be the subject of a book, I would have emphatically replied, "no way, not Mom, not Jean Duggan Entress." She lived an ordinary life, never seeking nor desiring attention for anything about herself. She was truly content and joyful being a wife, mother, and Godly woman.

The twists and turns life takes, especially when God is at the helm, are astounding. Jean's story is an example, among countless others in history, of how God works through ordinary people in unforeseen ways when we have our yes on the table for Him. I thank each of the following for being a part of our journey.

To Mom, I could not love you more. I think about you each day and continue to stand amazed at your faith and humbled that God blessed me with such an inspiring mother, role model, and friend.

To Dad, who chose Mom for his wife after three months of knowing her, you could not have picked a better wife for yourself and mother for us. You are the wisest and most loving man I know and the best Dad in the world. I thank God for you.

To Judy and Mark, you two are a gift from God, with your friendship, your always being there, your encouragement, compassion, the laughter you bring when we are together, and your many contributions to this work. This includes an extra thank you to Mark for helping Dad with the introductory letter he wrote for this book.

To Jerry, thank you for your encouragement and for your feedback on drafts. Thank you also for your beautiful artwork on this book's cover and the photographs within the book. What a God-given talent you have.

To Pam, thank you for being the world's best friend, always strong in faith and full of love in action. I am incredibly grateful for the evenings you took to review this book. Your comments, edits, and suggestions were extremely helpful.

To extended family and friends, thank you from the bottom of my heart for all of your prayers, cards, telephone calls, and visits. You kept us encouraged. You reminded us we are loved. We could not have done it without you.

To the staff at Strong Memorial Hospital, thank you for the diagnosis; it devastated us but your utmost professionalism and great compassion made it easier to bear and will always be remembered.

To the staff, chaplains, and volunteers at St. John's Home, thank you for the care you gave my mother—the compassion, the prayers, the music, and the friendly faces in the hallways. What you did for us, and what you do day in and day out, is immeasurable.

To my coworkers at the University at Buffalo Regional Institute, I am incredibly appreciative for your support and the flexibility that allowed me to be away from the office and with my mother during this time in her life. Thank you very much.

Lastly, to Jesus, thank you for Your love, Your sacrifice, for making God known to us, and for offering hope that transcends sickness and death. I look forward to seeing You face to face when You call me home. May this book and my life glorify Your name and make much of You.

Contents

Forward by Richard G. Entress.................................1

Introduction..4

Chapter 1: It Began With a Fall..............................9

Chapter 2: A Diagnosis, A Prayer.........................19

Chapter 3: Between Here and There....................26

Chapter 4: Fear and Faith..................................35

Chapter 5: Eyes For God...................................41

Chapter 6: Angels On Earth...............................47

Chapter 7: Love's Function................................51

Chapter 8: Beautiful Character, Imperfect Love........61

Chapter 9: Going Downhill, Called Upward...........66

Chapter 10: Home at Last..................................72

Epilogue...79

Letters From Mom..84

Resources...97

Notes..99

FORWARD BY RICHARD G. ENTRESS

Me? I am a lucky man, a very blessed person by really any measure. This is true even though I recently lost my beloved wife of forty-nine years. She was my beautiful partner. She is the woman who was a loving wife, caring mother to our three children, and a faithful follower of Jesus. She was a pillar of strength in many ways, and I miss her dearly.

Not long ago, my wife, Jean Entress, was diagnosed with amyotrophic lateral sclerosis. ALS is what it is often called. Five months later, I held her hand as Jean took her last breath. This book, written by our daughter, Sharon Ana, recounts my wife's last months, days, and final hours.

ALS is a debilitating disease. It slowly kills nerve cells affecting the muscles and leaves the body paralyzed. In this book, you will read about how this terrible illness progressed within my wife, and how this dire situation gave way to a beautiful demonstration of elegance, grace, and faith.

You probably picked up this book for a reason. Maybe you or a loved one was recently diagnosed with a serious illness. Maybe you have some health issues and are becoming less independent. Or maybe you have lost a loved one like me. *Sunny Skies From The Valley* is a gentle inspiration to not lose faith.

Faith in our family did not come by way of perfection. In our forty-nine years together, marriage was difficult at times. We saw our share of disease, addiction, and pain. However, we worked hard, fought for our family, kept our faith in God, and always did what we thought was right. I would not have changed a thing.

Looking back, I cannot help but feel proud. Not because everything was always great. Not because everything was perfect. We weren't living rich and worry free by any means. My pride is in my family's resilience to weather the storms and to always stand tall knowing that old adage "this too shall pass." Jean, the beloved matriarch of our family, set a very good example for us to follow.

My daughter has written *Sunny Skies From The Valley* to give a little bit of my wife's wisdom to the rest of the world. Jean was too modest to have ever written a book about herself, but her attitude and actions spoke loudly.

What Sharon Ana saw in Jean, and what she perceived of God's presence in our midst, she took note of, and wanted to share with you. A devout Catholic who loved Jesus and who always prayed for her children to love Him too, Jean would be proud of Sharon Ana for taking the opportunity to share the message of hope that you will find in this book.

With peace and faith,

Richard G. Entress

Our Family

Back Row: Sharon Ana, Mark, Mom, Judy, and Dad.
Front Row: Grandma B

A mother at heart, family pictures show Mom beaming more brightly on our special days than on her own. This one was taken at the University at Buffalo in May 2000 at my graduation from law school.

INTRODUCTION

Even though I walk through the valley of the shadow of death, I will fear no evil, for you are with me...

PSALM 23:4

Amyotrophic lateral sclerosis is commonly known as ALS or Lou Gehrig's disease. It is named after the New York Yankees Hall of Famer who was diagnosed with ALS in 1939. He passed away less than twenty-four months later at the age of thirty-seven.[1]

This rare disease is fatal. While up to five percent of those diagnosed with ALS will live at least twenty years after the onset of their symptoms, most survive two to five years after symptoms appear and a diagnosis is made, becoming progressively paralyzed over time.[2] The disease destroys muscle-controlling motor neuron cells in the brain and spinal cord that trigger voluntary movement throughout the body in the arms, legs, fingers, toes, vocal cords, face, and diaphragm. Victims become prisoners inside their own body, with their mind left largely intact.

Nobody knows exactly what causes ALS. Nine out of ten cases are sporadic. They occur without any known reason, although there are risk factors. These include age, being a veteran of war, male gender, head trauma, regular exposure to formaldehyde, lead exposure, and cigarette smoking.[3] The rest of cases—about five to ten percent—are genetic, passed from parent to child.[4] The genes that cause ALS are dominant. This means that it takes only one bad gene from a single parent to pass from one generation to the next.

ALS is a cruel, crippling disease that recently impelled lawmakers in Colorado to introduce legislation allowing physician-assisted suicide.[5] In California, an ALS patient was among the first to take advantage of a new state law, passed in June 2016, allowing doctor-assisted suicide.[6] The disease is also among the conditions Canada's highest court recently considered in ruling that doctors cannot be barred from helping patients with "grievous and irremediable conditions" such as ALS end their lives to avoid unbearable suffering.[7]

I mention this not because I am an advocate of physician-assisted suicide. I am not. However, this movement sheds light on the insidious nature of the disease Mom faced. It is one where a growing number of states and countries consider hastening death as the most humane way of handling it. I suppose it is oftentimes hard to imagine how life with grave suffering can have inordinate value and make an immeasurable and long-lasting impact.

***

Perhaps the cross that miraculously appeared in the window of Mom's hospital room during the early morning hours back in May 2014 was a sign that what landed her in the hospital called for a visible reminder of God's great love. At the time, none of us suspected anything serious, certainly not anything life threatening. That cross, however, was a harbinger of things to come.

A diagnosis came later that week. Mom had amyotrophic lateral sclerosis. For our family, the disease was a test of faith like no other. I, Jean's eldest daughter, questioned how God allowed this to happen to someone who loved Him so much. We enlisted family and friends to pray for a miracle. Mom, meanwhile, continued to believe in the Lord's goodness and power, even in the midst of the diagnosis. "God has shown me many miracles over the years," she once confided in me.

Mom was a friend of God from a young age. She was the middle child in a family of seven, with two older brothers, Bill and Richard, and two younger sisters, Patricia and Maureen. Her parents named her Jean, of Hebrew origin, meaning "a gift from God." Almost as if her first name said it all, describing her character in full, Jean had no middle name. And she seemed to know her origin, almost instinctively, as a child. Mom's faith and love for God were remarkable. "When we were young, your mother preferred being in church than playing outside with friends," says her younger sister Pat. "I didn't understand that," she adds. As a teen, Jean considered becoming a nun.

As an adult, Jean never forgot her roots. She grew up poor, three girls to a bedroom and one new outfit a year. Easter was the season when the family went clothes shopping. Growing up frugally impacted Mom. For as long as I can remember, if my mother purchased something new, she donated something old, or she couldn't sleep well at night. She felt she had more than she needed and something somebody else could use.

Always forefront in Mom's mind was doing the right thing in the sight of God. Within her was a strong moral compass, grounded in the Bible. Mom threw the world's ways to the wind. She lived humbly, splurged rarely, and regularly attended church and confession. She wouldn't drink and didn't swear. She did her utmost best to pass along these and many other values to us, her children, who could be a bit unruly and rebellious at times.

"I remember the Monday morning Mom called me at work," recalls Judy, the middle child in the family.

"Judy, I have something to tell you."

"What Mom?" Judy asked, dreading the worst. "Mom never called me at work, unless it was urgent."

"I don't want you and Mark watching Saturday Night Live at the house anymore. I don't like what I hear."

"I was in my thirties," Judy adds, "living on my own."

Always the family peacemaker—typical of her middle child standing—Judy elaborates on her position and Mom's:

I can understand how Mom was offended. The show is funny but the humor is coarse. I don't watch it any longer. I used to tape it and bring it over to the house because Mark liked it. It was something to do after dinner. We didn't watch it in the living room where Mom and Dad sat. We were downstairs in the family room but not out of earshot. Mom heard. She always had good ears. And this wasn't the first time she said something to me about that show. I didn't object when she called. It was their house. I just couldn't believe Mom was calling me at work on a Monday morning to tell me to not watch a TV show. She felt that strongly about it.

Her heart was pure. Mom saw God more clearly than us or anyone we knew, His extraordinary power in the ordinary of everyday life. My inbox is filled with e-mails from Mom, letters of miracles, stories of faith, thank you notes, and encouraging words full of grace and gratitude. I could bring a small loaf of plain bread to Thanksgiving dinner, and Mom would send me the nicest thank you note from her and Dad, telling me how delicious the loaf was and how everyone enjoyed it so much. After holiday celebrations, she snail mailed thank you letters, individual ones to each of us. These were handwritten notes, perfectly penned and often on cards she received from supporting missions work in the world. Her gratitude for even the smallest things cultivated generosity in those around her.

Prayer requests in our family went to Mom. A prayer warrior, she took all concerns, worries, and special requests to God.

"You can pray too," she sometimes said to me.

"I know, Mom. I do. But I don't know if I have the direct line to God that you do."

Mom smiled in response. Meanwhile, I quietly wondered whether our family was as blessed as it was because of Mom's dedication to prayer and her closeness to God.

Yet, as Mom's faith and prayers inspired and protected us over the years, Lou Gehrig's disease waged war on her body. It began taking her ability to walk, move, swallow, and breathe. What happened to her outsides brought buckets of tears, grief, and fear. It also produced unexpected joy and blessing. God showed up during times when we least expected, giving us strength, stronger faith, a larger, eternal perspective, and practical provision for day-to-day needs. God tells us that His power is made perfect in our weakness. Mom's condition offered vast and fertile ground for Him to work. I witnessed it from day one.

I told Mom this book would be our ministry together. It is my prayer—our prayer—that this account, factual and accurate to the best of our recollection, points readers to God whose power is made perfect in our weakness. Our Heavenly Father weeps with us in our sorrow. His peace transcends understanding, and He loves each of us beyond measure. It is something we can be sure of, even when we are in one of life's valleys.

CHAPTER 1
It Began With A Fall

CHAPTER ONE

It Began With A Fall

...I was given a thorn in my flesh.... Three times I pleaded with the Lord to take it away from me. But he said to me, "My grace is sufficient for you, for my power is made perfect in weakness."

2 CORINTHIANS 12:7-9

Nothing about Mom's disposition hinted at anything threatening. She was in good spirits, almost cheerful, when I visited her in the hospital that afternoon back in May 2014. I took off work early that day to make the hour and a half drive from downtown Buffalo to the hospital where Mom was admitted in Rochester, New York. I approached her side of the hospital room, near the window, with flowers and candies in hand from the gift shop downstairs. Her jaw dropped as our eyes met and quickly transformed into the widest smile. "Ana! What are you doing here?"

I had debated whether to visit Mom that afternoon. I traveled there two days earlier and did not think Mom would be in the hospital long. However, I am thankful now that I made that trip. It surprised her greatly. It made her day. And the opportunities to demonstrate how much I love her would soon grow slim.

"I came to visit you, Mom. I feel badly how you fell and are in the hospital days after our celebration." It was Monday, May 12, 2014.

It was the day after Mother's Day and less than a week after Mom's seventy-first birthday, when Mom fell to the ground in the bathroom at home. By this point, she was getting around in a wheelchair. She was unable to take more than a few steps on a walker without falling. While she had fallen in the past, Dad, a year her senior, was unable to help her up this time. He called 911. As Dad explains:

> She was on the ground, wedged between the toilet and the wall. I couldn't get her up with one pull. When she fell the other day, in the living room, I was able to get her up a little at a time. I lifted her a bit and put a cushion from the sofa under her. I lifted her a little more and added another cushion, until she was high enough to pull her to a stand. In the bathroom, there wasn't the room to work like that.

While Mom did not appear to break anything, she complained of shortness of breath. The two ambulance workers who responded to the call transported her to Strong Memorial Hospital, where they put her on the neurology floor, after a short stay in the emergency room.

The incident came after a precipitous decline in Mom's health over the preceding twelve months. Her first bad tumble happened in the parking lot of Wegmans grocery store in May of the previous year. She injured her head badly, falling backwards onto concrete. She was in the hospital several days, requiring stitches. They discharged her with an order for outpatient physical therapy to strengthen her bad knee, which they determined then was the cause of the fall.

Physical therapy was ineffective. We watched Mom go from using a cane, after the fall at Wegmans in late May, to a walker. By August, Mom could no longer manage the flight of stairs up to the bedroom, and Dad installed a chairlift in their two-story townhouse. As Dad remembers:

She couldn't make the last step at the top of the staircase where the railing ends. I was afraid she would fall backwards. I climbed the stairs behind her, holding the railings on both sides, pushing her up and preventing her from falling backwards, but she also needed someone in front of her at the top to pull her up that last step. There was just the two of us. She couldn't do it.

Soon Mom was in a wheelchair, and Dad wheeled her wherever she needed to go. Mom navigated just enough steps with a walker to make transfers, such as from her wheelchair to her chair in the living room. However, even this was difficult. Her feet did not respond the way she wanted them to. Turns were the worst. Her upper body turned with the walker, but her lower body did not always follow. Only occasionally did Mom and Dad leave the house together—for doctor's appointments, a meal out, or to visit Grandma B.

***

Grandma B was Dad's mother. B was short for Bernice, her first name. We called her Grandma B to distinguish her from her mother, our great grandmother, whom we called Grandma A. The A was short for Anna. It is where my middle name came from.

Grandma B was ninety-six years old, but decades younger than her chronological age in heart and mind. Unable to walk any longer herself—she had a bad sciatica nerve that became worse, as the years progressed—Grandma B was in a nursing home. She was transferred there from assisted living. She fell in exhaustion one evening. She was unable to make the trip from her bedroom to the dining room for meals, as they required of all residents. Her legs no longer moved. Before this, Grandma B lived independently and drove into her nineties, when she willingly gave up her driver's license to avoid being a danger to others on the road.

The move dampened her social life a bit. Grandma B was known at the local restaurant where she enjoyed stopping in for breakfast after church on Sunday mornings or for lunch. Most of the time, she went with friends or family, but she was also not averse to dining alone. Even being on a walker to get around, it did not stop Grandma B one bit from doing the things she loved to do. Dining ranked at the top of that list. Grandma B could eat almost as much as the men in our family could. She enjoyed a full course dinner, while Judy and I felt stuffed like a potato on a simple sandwich or breakfast food.

Nursing home life greatly depressed Grandma B, at least at first. She did not understand why God would not call her home, having lost her husband, the love of her life, decades earlier. She lost many of her close friends too. She even lived to lose one of her two daughters to cancer. It broke her heart, especially knowing that Aunt Marion, who was always full of life, energy, and enthusiasm, left a college-age daughter.

Ever so slowly, Grandma B did assimilate to nursing home life, and her spirits lifted as she came to know the staff and others there. This included Sam the mailman, as we all affectionately called him. Sam was there nearly every day visiting his wife, and he made an effort to get to know the other residents.

Sam was from Grandma B's town and familiar with the Entress name. A number of Entresses lived on Coldwater Road and the surrounding streets in the Gates Chili area, where Sam delivered mail. Coldwater Road is where my grandfather, Bernard Entress, grew up, the son of Engelbert and Mary Louise and the youngest among their eight children.

This connection established an instant and easy rapport and friendship between Sam, Grandma B, and our family. Every time I saw Sam in the hall, he would greet me with a smile, asking how I was doing and inquiring how Bernice was getting along.

In time, Grandma B became so well respected that she was elected president of the residents at her nursing home. Grandma B reluctantly accepted that title. Her face wrinkled up, and her head shook defiantly when she told me about it one day. Underneath the exterior, though, I believe a part of Grandma B felt honored to be seen as one of the most capable ones there, charged with being the eyes, ears, and voice of residents.

Eventually, Grandma B wholeheartedly embraced that role. It was an extension of the leadership roles she held throughout her life, being president of the Widows Club and, in her younger adult years, the Women's Alter Society at St. Helen's Church, where she and Grandfather attended. Grandma B was also the organizer of Sunday afternoon gatherings that brought together family, friends, and neighbors at their home at 25 Hartom Road in the Town of Chili, New York.

Their house was a four-bedroom ranch with a sprawling patio out back and a basement made for entertaining, with a piano, ping-pong table, and closet full of games. Grandfather built the home for his young and growing family in 1949. Grandma B's prized possession was the in-ground pool out back. One year, Grandfather sold a plot of land to install that pool for her. Even decades later, Grandma B never tired of telling the story about how Grandfather surprised her with the pool of her dreams.

At Grandma B's suggestion, windows throughout the nursing home were washed one spring, so the sunlight could more brightly shine in, and residents could better see out. An extra sausage link was added to the morning breakfast plates, when Grandma B brought to their attention that the menu specifically lists sausage links. "There is an "s" at the end," said Grandma. "We should get more than one link." Not only did Grandma B enjoy food, she was a stickler for following the rules.

Management put their foot down when Grandma B once suggested the place could benefit from electrical rewiring. She said something about the cords when I asked her where this new idea of hers came from. Grandma B thought she knew a thing or two about these matters, having been married to a homebuilder and being a do-it-yourself homeowner herself. Grandma B was, in fact, a truly modern day woman. She was independent, confident, and exceptionally capable in all she did.

***

Perhaps because of Grandma B's slower physical decline, which was tempered by doctor visits, chiropractor care, and a can-do attitude, we did not see nor feel the gravity of what Mom faced. We simply assumed she had osteoarthritis in her knee. She never complained about anything but a bad knee, for which she wore a knee brace, and shortness of breath. We reasoned the shortness of breath was from Mom getting out of shape from less and less physical activity.

She had gone for cardiopulmonary testing, to check the functioning of her heart. However, she passed with flying colors. Her doctor recommended that she see a neurologist next, to further explore what might be causing her symptoms, but Mom did not pursue it. She did not insist on the explanation and solution that I imagined for myself, if my mobility was impaired even slightly. She was at peace with accepting what came to pass.

With no diagnosis to warrant such a severe decline over this short time span, we blamed Mom and Dad, as Judy recounts:

> I thought Mom wasn't trying hard enough. I think we all felt she was letting this happen to herself, and Dad was enabling it. We didn't understand. A doctor told her after the fall at Wegmans that she needed a knee replacement. Yet Mom said she wanted to keep the knee God gave her. She didn't want to change the way God created her. Seeing her in a wheelchair, watching Dad do everything for her, was so upsetting. I purchased season tickets to the theatre, to limit my Sunday afternoon visits with them.

"I felt similarly," says Mark, our younger brother. "I was bewildered she wasn't taking steps to improve her situation. There was an accepting attitude that I didn't get. I felt there might have been a withholding of information too."

None of us realized the hurdles Mom faced or the extent of her burden, such as how she had numbness in her feet and legs and could not move or control her toes at all. We never knew how Dad lifted up her legs into bed at night, or how he helped her up out of bed in the morning. She and Dad quietly carried this burden gracefully, neither with an ounce of grumbling about how one or the other was managing more than their fair share of the load. Perhaps the only sign something more dreadful was happening to Mom's body was how she occasionally said to us, humbly, in her own defense, "You don't know what it's like to suffer." However, she never elaborated on that.

I pleaded with Dad on the phone one Monday night, less than two months before Mom's bad fall in the bathroom. "Dad, Mom is seventy years old and one step away from a nursing home. She needs physical therapy. She needs to move. If she doesn't move it, she is going to lose it, with the little mobility she has left."

Spurred on by this desperate plea, Dad called Mom's primary doctor the next morning. He arranged for in-home physical therapy. But it did not help at all. As Dad recollects:

> I sat here and watched the two of them do their thing. The physical therapist showed your mother how to roll a ball with her leg, as she sat in her wheelchair. She came out to the house a couple times a week, and it seemed to me, your mother was getting worse. There was no improvement. I kept thinking, "Why isn't this lady saying something?" I kept waiting for her to say something. I didn't want to say anything myself. I didn't want to discourage your mother, or she would have stopped the therapy immediately.

There were other symptoms too, but they were subtle and came on gradually. If we noticed, we brushed them off, attributing them to older age or lesser causes. Mom, for instance, was eating smaller amounts than usual and losing weight. At Bill Gray's restaurant, an egg sandwich and soup replaced the hamburger Mom used to order. The Mother's Day before she fell in the bathroom, she had less than a slice of pizza for dinner and the smallest sliver of cake, even though she always had a good appetite and a sweet tooth.

For lunch, she now did not eat more than a half sandwich, instead of her usual full. Dad thought he was overfilling the sandwiches again. It was a pet peeve of Mom's over the years. (Dad makes sandwiches restaurant style, while Mom spread tuna and other fillings on like butter.) Who could imagine Mom's ability to swallow was now compromised by a disease nobody yet knew she had?

Mom's voice was also getting softer, and she was talking less too. Dad later remarked how he had trouble hearing her, if he was talking to her from another room. He even gave her a bell to ring from bed, so she could get his attention, if he was downstairs. They woke at different hours. Dad was up before the birds. Three in the morning was common for him. Mom, on the other hand, generally woke up hours later, probably as the birds were lunching. When he heard her up, Dad headed upstairs to help her get ready for the day.

Our weekly telephone conversations grew short in the months preceding Mom's hospital admission. Frequently, she handed the phone over to Dad to talk to me after only ten minutes or so. A nagging but unfounded suspicion worried me that Mom was losing interest in talking with me after all of these years. I had no idea her ability to speak was slowly diminishing.

Before this, Mom and I regularly chatted for hours, sometimes until my phone battery went dead, especially if the conversation drifted to her life on Palm Street, where she grew up in the City of Rochester, or to God. Mom loved talking about Him. She often wondered what He thought of things going on in the world, or she shared with me a miracle she heard about.

Before I became a true believer in God, it was with more patience than passion that I engaged in these spiritual conversations with Mom. I remember mostly listening and mildly agreeing. After I became a believer, these conversations with Mom reflected a shared interest that greatly excited and encouraged us both. This change of heart took place in November 2007, when all doubts I had about God's existence evaporated. (This may be the subject of a second book.) During these later years, I remember being so thankful that God gave me parents who love the Lord and enjoy talking about Him as much as Mom did.

Yet, would Mom's faith or mine be strong enough to withstand the devastating news and grim diagnosis that her doctors would soon deliver to us all?

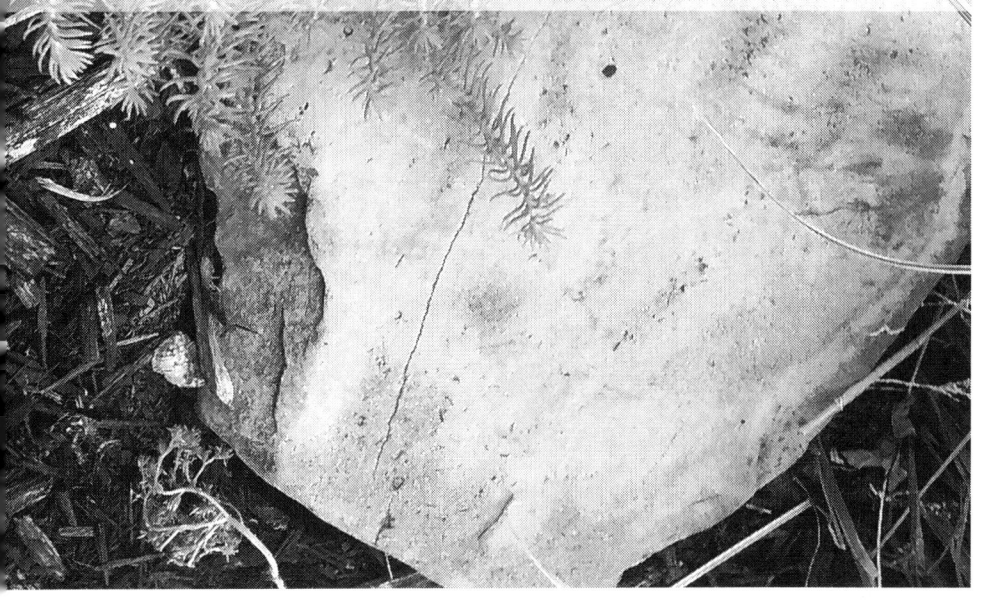

CHAPTER 2
A Diagnosis, A Prayer

CHAPTER TWO

A Diagnosis, A Prayer

Dear friends, do not be surprised at the fiery ordeal that has come on you to test you, as though something strange were happening to you. But rejoice inasmuch as you participate in the sufferings of Christ, so that you may be overjoyed when his glory is revealed.

1 PETER 4:12-13

When it came, the diagnosis hit us like an October snowstorm. I remember that Saturday, May 17 well. Judy and I went to Strong Memorial Hospital to visit Mom that afternoon. We planned to talk with her doctors. We wanted to ask them if they considered Parkinson's disease as the cause. With Mom in the hospital the entire week for testing, and not a hint from her doctors about what might be wrong, my siblings and I hoped we could help them out. We came prepared that day to point out possible symptoms and red flags that even we had overlooked until now. Looking back, her doctors wanted to be certain before sharing a diagnosis so ominous, findings they were prepared to give us that day.

It was there in the barren part of the hallway, on the neurology floor of Strong Memorial Hospital, that our world changed in an instant. Before we made our way into Mom's room, her nurse told us they have a diagnosis: amyotrophic lateral sclerosis. It is also known as Lou Gehrig's disease or simply "ALS." I do not remember anything said in the minutes after this. What stands in my mind is what the news did to my sister. She immediately broke down, crying uncontrollably, asking if they are sure.

While I was largely unaware at this point about what this disease is all about, my sister witnessed firsthand what it did to someone at her church:

> He was a handsome man with a family. He was in his later thirties or forties. I watched him go from leading his family into church, to using a cane, to eventually being wheeled in, in a Christopher Reeve kind of wheelchair, hooked up to oxygen. I later learned he had Lou Gehrig's disease. I knew there was no cure.

As I later learned, ALS paralyzes the body bit by bit, taking eventually one's ability to speak, swallow, and breathe. The mind is left largely intact, trapping one inside a useless body. The disease is fatal.

Visiting with Mom after this blow was tough. Her doctors came in and explained to us, as they had explained to her and Dad earlier that day, how they reached the diagnosis. Telltale signs included the muscle atrophy in Mom's legs and the slight twitches, called fasciculations, in the muscles affected by the disease. As Judy remembers, "They showed us Mom's legs, how her thighs were shaking. And her tongue... I went home that night and checked my own tongue."

The nerve cells in Mom's muscles were dying. The twitching stops when the nerve cells are dead and loss of any muscle strength is complete. The linchpin in their diagnosis was the results of Mom's heart and lung testing. Mom's heart, they said, was in perfect condition. Her lungs were in great shape too. But she took in only thirty percent of the oxygen a normal person her age breathed in, because the large muscle that expands and contracts the chest to let air in and out of the lungs—the diaphragm—was not responding as it should.

They explained how ALS is relatively rare. Only about two people out of every 100,000 get it.[8] There is no cure and only one drug that prolongs survival by a couple of months, on average, but only if it is taken during the earlier stages of the disease. "I'm beginning to see how powerful God is, that I got this," Mom interjected matter-of-factly.

"God didn't give this to you, Mom," I quickly reassured her. Although there wasn't an ounce of blame or negativity in what Mom said, I worried she would soon blame God for what this disease would do to her. She might go to her grave having lost faith, after being a tower of belief in our family.

As my sister and I continued to listen intently to her doctors, trying to digest it all and what it meant for Mom, we wanted to be strong for her. However, neither of us could stop crying. Mom was the strong one. I do not remember her shedding a tear, not for herself. Her eyes welled up with tears, only as she looked at us. It was out of compassion for the grief being experienced by her children.

"I knew then Mom was going to die," says Judy. "It was a death sentence." Compounding this was guilt. "Here Mom had this horrid disease, and to think we made life hard for her and Dad, questioning them the way we did. We were on them every week. We nearly blamed them for Mom's decline."

Dad says Mom had the same reserved reaction when she learned of the disease earlier that day. Her team of doctors shared with her and Dad how the disease would progressively worsen. Ultimately, ALS would take her ability to swallow and breathe. Her medical team suggested she get a tracheotomy and feeding tube inserted that week, life supports Mom immediately declined.

A mother at heart, she looked at us and said, "Don't cry. Don't feel bad for me. I think about what Jesus did on the cross. I can do a little suffering too." I could not believe my ears. How she could be so strong and at peace with the idea of suffering and with death? Where did this come from?

My mind flashed back to Easter Sunday. It was late that year, occurring on April 20, about three weeks before Mom's fall in the bathroom. After dinner, Mom shared with all of us how she watched the Passion of Christ that week. The movie depicts the suffering of Jesus in the days leading up to His crucifixion.

There was such sadness in her eyes and voice as she recounted what Jesus endured. He was betrayed by His friends, even Peter, the disciple who boasted he would die for Jesus. She told of how Jesus prayed to His Father for this cup to pass, if there was any other way. He was then flogged on his way toward Calvary, bearing the cross and ultimately crucified for the sins of humankind.

"She was crying. It was like the first time she ever saw it," remembers Judy. I remember tearing up myself as Mom described the story, touched by how she told it in her soft-spoken voice and remembering all of the details. It was not a movie star she was telling us about that evening, nor a storybook legend. Mom was reliving the sacrifice of her friend.

This friend, Jesus—God with skin on—He was the one who protected her at home when she was young, growing up with a father who struggled with addiction and was violent when he drank, lashing out at those he loved the most. He, the giver of good and perfect gifts, brought Dad into her life, an incredibly loving and faithful husband who proposed to her after three months of meeting her. He, the great physician and maker of miracles, was also the one who answered her prayers and miraculously healed me, their eldest daughter.

In and out of the hospital during my teenage years, sometimes for months at a stretch, nobody knew if I would live or die, or if life would ever return to normal. Yet Mom turned to God in prayer—

she even enlisted nuns from across the country to pray with her and Dad. And she clung to God's Word closely, enrolling in a Bible study at the church, so she could know Him better. It took some years, but that miracle came. Mom's prayers for my life, which hung on the line, were answered.

***

Back at home in Buffalo that Saturday evening, I called my friend Paige and told her about the diagnosis. She was keenly interested in hearing about how the visit went because she knew we suspected Parkinson's, a disease her mother has been living with for some years. "That's the worst diagnosis ever," she exclaimed when she heard Lou Gehrig's. A straight shooter who speaks from the heart, she told me the next day that she wept and prayed that night for Mom, even though she had never met her.

I could not sleep at all and tossed and turned all night. Weary and red-eyed at church the next morning, I begged God to tell me why He would allow my mother to deal with the worse disease ever. "She loves You," I pleaded. "She always tried to do the right thing in life." She and Dad brought us up to know and love You and walk in faith.

Several years earlier, Mom sponsored Judy, as Judy prepared to be confirmed in her faith at St. Anne's, the church she had attended for years. The process involved nearly a year of weekly meetings and studies.

"I absolutely needed a sponsor," explains Judy. "If Mom said no, I don't think I would have done it, and for me, being confirmed was life changing in unexpected ways."

The same year Judy was confirmed, Mom and Dad traveled to Buffalo to support me as I was baptized as an adult one Sunday morning at the non-denominational Christian church I had attended for several years. While I was baptized as a baby, I also lived apart from God for many of my adult years. I was so far apart from God, I used to tell people I was an atheist and did not believe that God existed. For me, adult baptism was an important outward expression of a newfound inner faith in God that came after much active searching and a conviction that God is real and that Jesus is my Savior.

Looking back, I can't help but think these milestones made Mom's heart smile. At the same time, she never gave up, lost hope, or poured out smaller amounts of love when the faith of her children was thin, if existent at all.

"Don't you love her, God?" is all I could ask. "Why did she get dealt such a bad hand?"

It was there in my distress, at the nine o'clock morning service, that God spoke to my heart. She does not have the worst diagnosis He told me. No, consider her faith. She has an eternal destiny, with Him, a future place in Heaven, that no disease, no calamity, nothing, can take away.

Yet, her disease frightened me. It took about one month before I typed the name of it into Google, to learn more about this vile illness. It took me this long even though I work at the university by day, and I am known to research things obsessively. Months before this, I spent an embarrassing number of hours learning everything I could about glaucoma. My visual field test at the eye doctor came back inconclusive, so they asked me to come back for retesting to rule out glaucoma, which they did.

"God we need You," I prayed, having traveled from my home church that Sunday morning after Mom's diagnosis to the Sisters of Saint Francis that afternoon. It was a convent I headed to, where my great aunt and grandfather's sister—Sister Bernard Marie Entress—used to be a nun. The church inside is open to the public and is a quiet, peaceful place to meditate in prayer. "God, please consider a miracle healing for Mom. If this isn't Your will at this time, I pray Mom continues to see You clearly and know how much You love her."

CHAPTER 3
Between Here and There

CHAPTER THREE

Between Here and There

*For we know that if the earthly tent we live in is destroyed,
we have a building from God, an eternal house in heaven,
not built by human hands.*

2 CORINTHIANS 5:1

Mom stayed at the hospital for a week after her diagnosis for some further testing. She was then transferred to the Highlands at Brighton for in-patient physical and occupational therapy. The short-term goal was for Mom to get strong enough so she could help herself get in and out of a wheelchair and take a few steps on her own. She would come home to live until she needed more intensive care.

Mom gave it her all, going for therapy twice a day. But as she tried to build up her strength, her muscles grew weaker. The nerve cells in her body continued to die, sending fewer and fewer signals where they were needed. Exacerbating matters, Mom became short of breathe with modest levels of exertion. She was unable to take in the air needed to do much more than peacefully sit in a chair and engage in sedentary activities such as watching TV, working on a jumble puzzle from the newspaper, or simply visiting.

"We could set up a hospital bed in your dining room, if there isn't a bedroom on the first floor, and you could purchase a home Hoyer lift or a sit-to-stand machine, similar to what we have been using here for transfers." After three weeks of therapy and little improvement, a decision had to be made about where Mom went from here, either back home or to a nursing home. We met with her medical team to discuss the options and the supports available to us if Mom came home. This included Dad, my siblings, and me. I arranged to take a leave of absence from work, move back to Rochester, and help Dad with Mom for as long as necessary.

"Go home and enjoy the rest of the summer; you aren't 'actively dying' right now," the nurse at the meeting table said to encourage Mom. She was unaware that Mom told Dad prior to the meeting that she didn't want to go home unless she was well enough to be there. In Mom's mind, this meant being able to walk at least a few steps on her own with the help of a walker, which she still was not able to do. They were using a sit-to-stand apparatus to assist Mom with transfers from one seating position to another. For Mom, this machine was a lifesaver, relieving her from having to rely on her legs and feet, which she could barely move.

While Mom was more receptive to the idea of going home by the end of this hour-long family meeting with her medical providers, this changed the very next day. As Dad tells it, "She didn't want to be cared for at home. She didn't want a bed in the dining room, or to see us dismantle the downstairs, replacing the carpeting with floorboards, to accommodate a lifting machine."

"Mom, why don't you want to come home?" I asked her when I visited next. I was unaware of what she told Dad. I worried she changed her mind to lesson the burden on me, even though helping to care for her is what I wholeheartedly wanted to do. "What happened?"

"It's not that I don't want to," she replied. "Sometimes you have to know when to let go." While I understood, I was disappointed by her decision. Judy, on the other hand, sounded unmistakably relieved when I talked with her.

"Taking care of Mom around the clock would be tough on us all, but especially Dad. We don't want to put him at risk. We can't lose Dad too."

Indeed, it was daunting, with Mom's many medical and personal care needs. Not one of us in the family had any hands-on medical experience. Insurance, we were told, covers an hour or two of in-home nursing care a week, but that was it for in-home assistance.

"But I know a woman who was confined to a wheelchair, paralyzed like Mom. She had an aide around the clock right in her home. I can't imagine she was wealthy. How did that happen?" I asked Mom's medical team. They indicated she might have had Medicaid, offering greater coverage than most private insurances for in-home services. I later learned that the paralyzed woman I knew received in-home assistance through a program for persons with traumatic brain injury.

***

St. John's Home was one of a handful of nursing homes recommended to us. We asked Mom's medical team for a short list of the best. I also scoured the ratings of nursing homes in our area using the U.S. government website called *Nursing Home Compare*.[9]

We made an appointment to tour St. John's, the one closest to home, and explore its fit for Mom. Located across the street from Olmsted-designed Highland Park, home of the annual Lilac Festival, I was impressed as soon as we entered with how welcoming the place is to visitors. Beyond the reception desk and sign-in sheet is a beverage bar for guests: coffees, teas, hot chocolate, and punch. "Grandma B's nursing home is nice, but nothing like this," I immediately thought to myself.

"It was like the Marriot," says Dad of his initial impression. A builder by trade, he adds, "It's a great big masonry building, well constructed of brick and stone."

Founded in 1889 by several churches[10], St. John's is today one of the largest nursing homes in the area with over 450 beds. Their first facility was on Lake Avenue, in the city, about two miles from where Mom grew up. They moved to their current location near Highland Park near the turn of the twentieth century. At that time, horticulturist and philanthropist George Ellwanger, an immigrant from Germany, donated his mansion to the home. St. John's Home bears the name of Saint John, a disciple of Jesus. John was one of the twelve and known as "the disciple whom Jesus loved" (see John 13:23, 19:26, and 20:2, as examples).[11]

God worked through Saint John to share Himself with the world through the written word. Divinely inspired, Saint John wrote several books of the New Testament in the Bible. Saint John also looked after Mary, the mother of Jesus, in her older years. Saint John took Mary into his home, and he cared for her as his own mother, at the command of Jesus:

> Near the cross of Jesus stood his mother and his mother's sister....When Jesus saw his mother there, and the disciple whom he loved standing nearby, he said to her, "Woman, here is your son, and to the disciple, "Here is your mother." From that time on, the disciple took her into his home. (John 19:25-27)

At St. John's, Natalie from the admissions office greeted us warmly and showed us around. On the ground floor, we saw a gorgeous outdoor courtyard that any horticulturist, even one as famous as Ellwanger, would be proud of. Thick vegetation and an assortment of flowers abounded. It is a place where residents can visit their family and where concerts are held during the summer. The space boasts a gazebo and a glider that accommodates wheelchairs.

Indoors are a volunteer-run gift shop and an old-fashion ice cream parlor with a jukebox and seventy-five cent sundaes. Down different halls from here is a large, indoor auditorium for resident events, a dentist office, hair salon, barbershop, and business offices.

Natalie then led us up to the third floor of an older attached building where St. John's chapel and spiritual department are located. A winding pathway from this leads to a cafeteria for staff, residents, volunteers, and visitors. Residents eat there free.

We then followed Natalie up to the third floor, to the resident area, in one of their newer wings. As the doors of the elevator opened, we stepped out into the midsection of the space. The area was a hub for residents, especially after meals. Looking out of the elevator, I immediately felt a sense of disappointment. I later learned Judy did too. As she recalls:

> It looked like a nursing home to me. The luxury downstairs wasn't up here, at least not in the people. Not that they weren't happy. The alert ones seemed to be. I noticed them smiling. But it was sad to think Mom had to be here. But this was before we got to know the other residents. Getting to know them changed things a lot.

Marching forward, we continued our tour, following Natalie straight ahead into the lunchroom and kitchen area. Here, residents order what they want to eat when they come in for meals, not days in advance as in some nursing homes. It was a homey area, set up with over a dozen small tables throughout the room, a large screen TV at one side, and a variety of potted plants lining the entire window sill across the back.

Natalie then showed us an empty resident room, near the end of a hallway bearing a plaque that read, "Life is not about how many breaths you take, but about the moments that take your breath away." The space impressed Dad. As he remembers:

> The rooms are designed for lifts; all of the doors are wide enough, even the bathroom door. And the bathrooms are spacious enough to fit a lift. You can get the machine inside and close the door behind

you. They did not need to use commodes in the room, as in other nursing homes. It was a nice point.

Each side of the room had a window that opened and closed, and each resident had control over the air temperature on their side, with air conditioning or heat. On the wall outside every bedroom was a picture of the residents inside and a note about them and their life: family, hobbies, travels, past jobs, and favorite things. "Seeing this reminded me these are people like you and me," observes Judy.

As we continued to look around and headed back downstairs, I drilled Natalie with a list of questions I had brought:

What is the menu selection for people who can't chew well? Are there call bells in every room and bathroom? Are you experienced in treating ALS patients? What special services do you offer for those who lose their ability to talk? What kind of lifting machines do you use? How many do you keep on each floor? Do you accept Medicaid, when the insurance and savings run out?

"I can tell how much you all love your mother, by all of the questions you asked," Natalie later said to me, as I ran into her one afternoon on my way upstairs to visit my mother. St. John's is the home we selected for her. We did not look at any others. And by the grace of God, that empty room Natalie showed us remained vacant while all of Dad's paperwork was processed.

***

Mom liked it there, especially as she became familiar with the routine and got to know the staff and other residents a bit. Her room on the third floor faced the courtyard below. From Mom's bed, you could look forward and see the sky, "God's sky," as she always called it.

Mom enjoyed watching the birds fly past her window as she lay in bed. We noticed how they gathered and perched themselves along the building perimeter when it rained outside. These little creatures have an innate ability to weather the storms of life by anchoring themselves in the company of each other. More amazingly, they do this before the rain and wind hit, almost as if they receive an airborne telegram, warning them to prepare for adversity.

Mom shared her room with a lovely woman named Jane who looked years younger than her age. Jane had a big smile, white teeth, reddish brown hair, and a sense for fashion. Across the hall from Mom and Jane, in a single room laid out as a studio apartment, was a couple married nearly eighty years and still going strong.

Also strong was St. John's responsiveness to Mom's medical needs. On the day she arrived, they had a bed there for her with a state-of-the-art air mattress, designed to treat and prevent pressure sores. People like my mother who can't move or shift their weight from one side to another on their own are at high risk for getting these pressure sores.

Weeks after her arrival, they delivered a big beautiful brown recliner to Mom's room, when my mother told them she might prefer reclining in a chair during the day rather than in bed. She also received an entirely new wheelchair when a visit to the ALS clinic at Strong Memorial Hospital determined the chair she had was slightly too big for her diminishing frame. On the occasions Mom needed to see a specialist, they frequently came to see her that day.

"The staff were competent," says Mark, our brother the businessman who pays compliments sparingly. "They did a good job, from what I saw. They didn't just put food in front of her at meals. There was attention paid to how much she was eating, if she was eating, and how she was eating."

"It was more like a hospital," declares Dad.

As nice as the place was in many ways, it was not the forever home Mom longed for. She saw it as a stomping ground of sorts between here and there. In the dining room at lunch one day, about a month after Mom moved in, the conversation among her lunch mates turned to how they preferred to be back in the homes they came from. With her husband sitting by her side, Mom's roommate Jane said she is trying to get well enough to go back home.

Mom then boldly announced, "My next home will be Heaven." Then, almost as if to not sound overly confident, as all eyes at the table turned to her, Mom added, "I hope." That hope Mom had of a Heavenly home was later rewarded when God gave her a glimpse into what He had for her.

CHAPTER 4
Faith and Fear

CHAPTER FOUR

Faith and Fear

For the Spirit God gave us does not make us timid, but gives us power, love and self-discipline.
2 TIMOTHY 1:7

"How is your mother doing?" Jane asked me one evening, after Mom and I returned to the room after dinner. On most days, Jane joined us in the dining room. However, she recently broke a bone and was confined temporarily to bed.

With many residents on the third floor of St. John's unable to carry on even a short conversation, Jane was a great blessing to Mom and our family. She was youthful and caring, a people-person at heart, and a great conversationalist. Jane usually came to dinner with a question on her mind. "Do you know what is playing on Broadway?" she asked me once. Another time, "Why do you suppose homes likes these have a bad reputation?" Our table had such interesting and lively dinner conversations. Many times, we lingered long after everyone finished eating and were the last ones to leave the dining room.

It was an easy and natural friendship. Jane and Mom had something considerable in common, namely, incredibly faithful and loving husbands. Jane's husband Dick visited almost every day, like Dad who did not miss a beat in being there for Mom. And the two couples—Dick and Jane and Dick and Jean—enjoyed lunch together with the others in the dining room nearly every day.

Before her recent injury, when Jane was more mobile, she would sometimes wheel herself into Mom's side of the room to visit while I was there. I remember one conversation when the three of us talked for nearly an hour about everything under the sun: fashion, relationships, marriage, family, Jesus, and Heaven.

At one point, I remember seeing Jane gaze at Mom, astounded that she never liked to wear earrings or colorful sneakers. "Jean, you really would have made a good nun." Jane heard how Mom considered becoming a nun before she met Dad.

On this one evening, however, as Jane inquired about Mom from her bed, she added how badly she felt that Mom has such a terrible disease. By this point, in early August, the disease had taken much from Mom. Lying in bed, my mother could turn her head from left to right, or she could move her arms and fingers enough to grab hold of and press the nurse call cord. The cord was always within reach, either secured to her clothing with a clip, when she was in bed, or near her wheelchair.

Swallowing was becoming noticeably more difficult too. Mom could not eat anything too thick or too thin, or she choked. There was actually a scare in the cafeteria, as we ate dinner there one night, just the two of us, for a change of scenery. Thank goodness the choking passed. I didn't know the Heimlich maneuver. Even Mom said she was afraid for a second she was going to choke to death. Afterwards, the staff required her to eat on the floor in the lunchroom, so they could keep an eye on her and assist as necessary.

Although Jane was now bedridden from her fracture and in some pain herself, she felt worse for Mom, knowing that she herself would heal in six to eight weeks. Mom's condition would likely continue to worsen. "I don't know how your mother got that disease. I hope you and your sister don't get it too."

I stood there stunned. Jane's comment was surely innocent enough and well meaning, but in my mind, it grew a deadly seed that had already been planted. After Mom's diagnosis in May, I fielded inquiries from family and friends, questions such as: "Is Lou Gehrig's hereditary? Does it run in families? Isn't there a genetic component?"

Back at the hospital, Mom's doctors asked whether anyone in the family ever had the disease. In five to ten percent of cases, genetics play a key causal role. "No, nobody," we quickly replied. However, Mom's parents and a couple of her siblings died young, from other causes. Who knows what diseases they might have faced had they lived longer.

For someone like myself who was always active and struggled to sit still for even a thirty-minute show on television, or a movie, the idea that I, too, might become totally paralyzed seemed like a nightmare.

But I didn't share this fear with Jane. I replied to her matter-of-factly. "I pray neither of us get it too, Jane. But if that is God's will, to allow that to happen, I will need to conform my will to His and trust that He will be my strength in my weakness. That is what it means to walk in faith and not according to our own ability."

There was silence for a moment as those words, conveying more confidence than I felt inside, resonated through Jane's half of the room. "That is difficult to do," Jane finally responded.

"Yes, I know it is. But I believe with God anything and everything is possible."

As I drove home to Buffalo that evening, I ruminated over that conversation and prayed that God would take away the fear I felt about my future. If I let it, that worry could have a stronghold on the rest of my life, something I knew would not honor Him. He tells us nearly countless times in His Word to us in the Bible not to worry about "what ifs" or fear things that may or may not happen.

From God's perspective, the only healthy fear is fear of God Himself.

As I continued to drive home, some of God's Words on the topic rushed through my mind:

> "Do not be anxious about anything, but in every situation, by prayer and petition, with thanksgiving, present your requests to God." (Philippians 4:6)

> "The Lord is my helper; I will not be afraid." (Hebrews 13:6)

God impresses on us to not fear because it is impossible to be filled with fear and walk boldly in faith. Indeed, fear implies a lack of trust in God's promises to provide for our needs, help us in our trials, and provide strength when we are weak.

In the days that followed, He reminded me of the people of Israel who spent much longer in the wilderness than God wanted for them. They lived on the edge, outside the Promised Land. Their fear and doubt in marching forward according to His will stopped them from entering and realizing the blessings God had prepared for them (see Numbers 14).

What a stark contrast to young Mary, the mother of Jesus. She could have easily been consumed with worries about her future too, having been informed by an angel of God that she would conceive by the power of the Holy Spirit. Who would believe her? Might Joseph decide not to marry her? Would he assume she was unfaithful to him? Would she live with the stigma of being an unwed mother? Might she be stoned to death, accused of having relations outside of marriage? It was an offense punishable by death at the time.

If Mary dwelled on these possibilities, these worst-case scenarios might have immobilized her in responding positively to God's call. Thankfully, Mary did not allow her mind to go down a pathway of doubt. Rather, she responded courageously in declaring, "I am the Lord's servant…May your word to me be fulfilled" (Luke 1:38).

My mother is another good example of one who did not live in fear of what might come to pass. She continued to trust in God's goodness, even when her circumstances were less than desirable. When friends commented on how terrible it was that she got this disease, she immediately turned the conversation to her own mother, who endured years of hardship with a husband—Mom's father—who battled addiction, was violent at times, and died young. Grandma Duggan was left to raise their children alone, even though she never worked outside the home during all of their married years, and was by then well along in years.

As for Mom, not once did she ask "why me" or question why God allowed her to deal with this disease and not yet perform the miracle so many of us prayed for. Written on Mom's mind and heart, as if to offer protection to the end, was the faithfulness of God, evident not only over the history of time, but throughout her own life.

One of the medical students at Strong Memorial Hospital who helped to diagnose Mom and who visited her almost every morning during her stay later wrote a beautiful note to our family. "I will remember her always," she penned. "She was a truly amazing woman, filled with love and always smiling… she would always have a story for me about how special her family was to her and how her faith in God has gotten her through everything."

CHAPTER 5
Eyes For God

CHAPTER FIVE

Eyes for God

Blessed are the pure in heart, for they will see God.

MATTHEW 5:8

One of Mom's favorite places at St. John's was the Chapel, located on the first floor of the South Building. For Dad, myself and my siblings, one of the big draws of St. John's was the spiritual support they offer, with weekly Mass, a team of active and caring chaplains, weekly Bible studies, and the opportunity to receive daily Communion.

Mom took advantage of many of these amenities, and she very much enjoyed visiting the Chapel. Outside of Sunday Mass, she asked to go there at other times during the week to look around. When her sister Pat visited in July, we took her to the Chapel a couple of times, at Mom's suggestion.

It was a beautiful, calming place, with stained glass windows in the front, a prominent cross at the head of the alter, a book for prayer requests, and a large-print Bible. Instead of the pews one finds in most churches, a large open area accommodated the many who came in wheelchairs for Sunday services.

Around the perimeter of the room were various statues and paintings. There was, for instance, a statue of St. John, the close friend and disciple of Jesus, who authored the fourth Gospel as well as four other books in the New Testament in the Bible. Across the room, there was a painting of Jesus' last supper. It showed Jesus enjoying Communion with his closest friends and followers, and giving thanks to God even when He knew His death was approaching. Nearby this was a statue of Mary holding baby Jesus. I remember Mom looking at this one and saying, "He is so beautiful."

A prominent picture of Jesus hung on the wall of the Chapel too. When we passed it, Mom often said, "There is God."

"Yep, that's Jesus, God with flesh on," I replied in response.

Mom's eyes were keenly fixed on Him. I remember stopping at the Chapel one evening before heading to the cafeteria to pick up some dinner that we would take back to the dining room on my mother's floor. As I wheeled Mom around the Chapel, looking at everything there, she pointed, "Look, they moved the picture of God!" Indeed, someone moved it from the side wall to the back wall.

What embarrassed me is what I thought to myself: "Would I have even noticed this had Mom not pointed it out?"

Even though Mom's memory was failing her a bit, to the point where she was taking notes on her favorite TV channels, past home addresses, and telephone numbers, her mind never lost track of Jesus. Mom had eagle eyes for Him. She always did.

I remember our second home as a family, a house that my grandfather built on Berna Lane, and the one I lived in when my younger brother was born. I was eleven years old when we moved there. Some years later, Mom discovered an image of Jesus etched in the woodwork on the closet door in the family room. She told us unceasingly how she loved looking over to that door from her chair, always reminded that God was there with her and the family.

Knowing the joy and comfort it brought to Mom, I felt sad for her when they decided to downsize and move into a smaller place. I vaguely remember suggesting that they take the door with them, but Mom was not keen on that idea. She trusted God was with them, door or not. And He was.

Not long after they moved, I remember Mom being so excited to share with me how she found another image of God. This time it was in the grain of the wood of their headboard. They owned that headboard on their bed since they were married decades ago, a gift to them from my grandparents.

Nobody noticed anything unusual about it until the movers mentioned the pattern in the wood. Mom studied it closely. She saw the face of Jesus. She and Dad showed me when I visited. I remember not seeing Jesus in the wood as clearly as she did, but that did not matter. Mom's sight was authentic.

She saw Him everywhere. She found Him not only in woodwork, but also in the miracles she believed in; in the lives of saints she loved reading about; in His Word to us in the Bible that she studied; and in nature. At dinner one night at St. John's Home, Jane explained how she would probably have stronger faith if she witnessed more miracles, such as during the time of Jesus.

"Look outside," Mom responded. "Look at the sky, the sun, the flowers, and trees. Man didn't make those." Mom saw them as beautiful creations of God, miracles of nature that pointed to a Creator, to God.

Jesus tells us that the pure in heart are blessed because they will see God. This was Mom, pure in heart. Her eyes for Him were so good because her heart was undivided with love for God. She wanted what He wanted. Humble in spirit, she did not have any agenda apart from Him. In fact, I cannot think of a single issue where Mom and God butted heads.

I continued to pray that if God chose not to miraculously cure her, Mom would at least continue to see Him clearly and feel His love for her. And I praise Him for answering this prayer.

It was Sunday, September 14 when Dad announced to me on our way to Sunday afternoon Mass with Mom that she had something to tell me.

"What's that?" I asked eagerly.

"I'll tell you after church," Mom replied quite nonchalantly.

By the time Mass ended, I nearly forgot about the cliffhanger she left me with. She didn't, though. As we sat there in the Chapel after the service—Mom in her wheelchair and I in a chair to her left—she asked if I wanted to hear what happened to her.

"Yes, of course. Tell me. What happened?"

The story that unfolded was an extremely emotional one for us both. She teared up before she even got to the heart of the matter. I recall being filled with fear, at least momentarily. I worried that perhaps something horrible happened to Mom. Her eyes were filled with water. She had a hard time articulating what she wanted to say, as if something inexpressible occurred.

Seeing her in this state, I got teary-eyed myself. I leaned over, hugging her, and asking her if she was okay. "Yes," she answered.

"What happened to you?" I pleaded softly. By this time, I wanted and needed to know.

"I saw God," she announced.

"You did? Where did you see Him?" I asked, filled with joy as well as relief. She proceeded to explain how she saw Him the other day out of the corner of her left eye, when she was in the bathroom in her room upstairs. She said she saw Him for a few seconds, but I could tell it created a memory that would last forever.

"What do you think of this, Mom?"

"It's wonderful," she answered.

I asked her what He looked like. She said like the picture of Jesus on the Chapel wall but darker.

"Mom, it looks like God wants you to know He is with you."

"I know He is with me," she firmly answered.

I have no doubt Mom felt excited and exceptionally blessed to see Jesus as she did during her lifetime, if even for a few fleeting seconds. Knowing this, I couldn't help but imagine what it will be like for her to realize the full fruition of her faith and see Him face to face and be with Him for eternity in Heaven.

CHAPTER 6
Angels On Earth

CHAPTER SIX

Angels on Earth

It is more blessed to give than to receive.

ACTS 20:35

"Do you work here at St. John's?" I asked the older gentleman standing behind the ice cream counter. This was back in June, before we selected St. John's for Mom. I dropped in on my own, on the way to visit Mom one Sunday, to check out the place and pick up any informational material they might have. I wanted to share with Mom the place we were considering for her, even before we met later in the week with the admissions staff for the tour.

"No, I volunteer here. My wife was here several years ago. After she passed away, I came back to volunteer." Later that summer Mom and I met a different gentleman in the auditorium who shared a similar story. He volunteered there with hospice patients. St. John's, in fact, boasts a small army of faithful volunteers that add immensely to the quality of life for residents and staff.

One of their most dedicated servants is Eddie. We got to know Eddie well, as he wears many hats. Some days he is chief transporter, making sure residents get where they need to go, both safely and promptly: to hair appointments, afternoon activities, and Mass on Sunday afternoons. Other days he is "Father Eddie" to some. No, Eddie is not a priest, but sometimes he is mistaken for one. He is a Eucharistic Minister who delivers Communion to any one of the hundreds of residents at St. John's who want it. Some, such as Mom, ask to receive Communion on a daily basis. Other days Eddie assists with bingo and other activities. He is also on the volunteer team that mans the ground floor ice cream shop, open from two to four in the afternoon. It is the only place in town that carries my favorite flavor: Peppermint Patty.

Eddie has been a volunteer at St. John's for nearly ten years. Some days, he is there all day, from morning to afternoon. He loves it that much. This is on top of his regular job and his service at his church in the city where Eddie sings in the choir and spends days volunteering at the annual second-to-new sale. "They call me Edverywhere," he says, "because I'm everywhere." "No" isn't a part of my vocabulary when it comes to lending a hand to those in need."

Yet Eddie is much more than a set of capable hands. He brings great joy, deep compassion, and wide smiles wherever he goes. He says his volunteer service repays him richly in six figures: S-M-I-L-E-S. Quick witted and outgoing, laughter happens easily when Eddie is around. "You've just celebrated your forty-ninth wedding anniversary, Mrs. Entress? Did you get married at six years old?" Eddie teased my mom, who grinned widely at the thought.

With his joyful disposition, one might suppose Eddie lived on top of the world for most of his life, carefree from the burdens that weigh a lot of us down. Yet, it was the opposite. The one who brings much joy to others endured more than his share of hardship and sorrow. He walks around with evidence of some of this. "I have an artificial knee, a knee of steel," he says, as he describes a biking accident he was in at the age of seventeen. A car backed up, knocking him off his bike, and injuring him pretty badly.

As a young husband and father of two, Eddie lost his wife to cancer. She was only in her thirties when God called her home. Singlehandedly, Eddie raised their two children. Then several years ago, he lost his parents, ten days apart. Within months of this, his brother suddenly passed away too.

"What makes you do this, Eddie? Why do you volunteer so much?" I asked him one afternoon when he stopped by to check on Mom, knowing from his morning visit that she had a very rough night. "God," He answered. "He showed me this is where I'm needed. Plus, I have a big heart, if you haven't noticed." (How could anyone not?)

As I walked in Delaware Park back at home in Buffalo one evening, I contemplated how one who has tolerated so much can be such a blessing to others—an angel—as Judy puts it. I considered how compassion and character often come from trials and suffering of many kinds. God's Word to us in the Bible tells us we have reason to rejoice when we find ourselves in a trial:

> We are full of joy even when we suffer. We know that our suffering gives us the strength to go on. The strength to go on produces character. Character produces hope. And hope will never bring us shame. (Romans 5:3-5, NIrV)

We can find joy not in the trial itself, but because of what the trying experience can produce in us. It cultivates qualities that directly benefit our lives and characteristics such as understanding and compassion, which God can work with, through us, to greatly bless others in need, just as He is doing right here at St. John's.

CHAPTER 7
Love's Function

CHAPTER SEVEN

Love's Function

Carry each other's burdens, and in this way you will fulfill the law of Christ.

GALATIANS 6:2

"Mom, what about St. John's do you enjoy the most?" It was a question I asked her one September afternoon, as she relaxed in bed. Two pillows propped up her head for easier breathing, as she lay there visiting with me. We both kept an eye on the clock hanging on the wall to the left of her window. We were eager for St. John's evening shift to arrive. Then, the aides assigned to Mom would come in to get her up.

It took two aides to lift Mom out of bed. As one carefully lifted her upper body, the other gently moved her legs and feet over the edge of the bed. From this sitting position, they put straps on Mom. These were used to position her securely into a lifting machine. The apparatus raised my mother into the air and took her wherever she was going, such as to the bathroom, or to her wheelchair. Hanging in mid air, Mom sometimes looked at me and hesitantly smiled. I suppose she wondered what I thought of the sight. Like her, I was thankful for the age we lived in with technology that enables paralyzed patients such as her to safely get around.

I shared with Mom how I was writing a book about her and this experience. "It will be our ministry together, Mom, to encourage others in their faith and help point them to God." Cheering Mom up was also on my agenda because she did not enjoy being in bed during the day, as her medical condition required.

As we passed time that afternoon, I considered with great wonder Mom's answer to the question I asked her, about her favorite thing at St. John's Home. Had Mom told me her favorite thing was church on Sunday afternoons, it would not have surprised me. Mom's strong faith and her love for going to church and communion since she was young showed consistently over the years and decades.

There was going to be no astonishment either if she said her favorite thing was events in St. John's large, ground-floor auditorium. A few weeks earlier, Judy and I took Mom to an Elvis concert in the auditorium. Mom was in her glory. Her eyes were so filled with joy that she was nearly moved to tears, hearing and singing along with the music she loved as a teenager.

However, neither of these claimed the number one spot. What did caught me off guard. "Going to the lunch room," Mom responded. As I later considered her answer, I knew it was by the sheer grace of God. This demonstrated His ability to provide in abundance for every occasion and difficulty.

That difficulty for Mom was eating. Her ability to swallow was markedly diminished. She could no longer enjoy many of her favorite foods such as bacon, lettuce and tomato sandwiches, or even a simple fruit cup. Staples these days included yogurt, pureed soup, mashed potatoes, oatmeal, ice cream and hot tea thickened with a squirt and a half of Simply Thick, a tasteless thickening agent.

As her disease progressed, meals could have easily become dreadful, but here my mother implied that meals were her most favorite thing. The company undoubtedly played a role. While my siblings and I took turns eating with Mom and the others at her table for dinner, Dad was present every day for lunch. His visits began mid morning and extended through the afternoon. He brought his lunch from home, the same thing every day: a yogurt, piece of fruit, and an unsweetened ice tea. Dad also enjoyed sampling what Mom received on her plate.

"The food was excellent," he recalls, "just like home cooking. One time your mother wanted my yogurt from home. I told her she could have it, but asked her to order the Reuben sandwich off the menu. We swapped. That sandwich was delicious, as good as you'd get in a restaurant."

Together, Mom and Dad enjoyed lunch with two other couples, Jane and her husband Dick, and the long-married couple from across the hall. Three different couples, all living out their vow, "for better or worse, for richer, for poorer, in sickness and in health, to love and to cherish, from this day forward until death do us part." I could not help but wonder if these lunches, which brought joy to Mom and a normalcy to her life, reminded her of when it all started with Dad. It was the meal that changed the trajectory of their lives. It was a story Jean never grew tired of telling.

***

They met in 1964 at a late-summer, picnic-style steak dinner in Powder Mill Park. The Saint Thomas Moore Club hosted the event. The Moore Club, as Mom often called it, was a group that brought together young Catholic single adults for social events and service. Mom and her sister Pat regularly attended together. Twenty-one years old, Mom had recently graduated from Nazareth Academy, an all-girls Catholic high school she attended because she wanted to become a nun. Aunt Pat recalls how Mom had strong faith from a young age. She genuinely enjoyed being in church, preferring that to playing outdoors with friends. However, at the time she met Dad, Mom was working as a teller at Central Trust Bank. She lived at home with her mother and younger sister Maureen. In the years preceding this, her father passed away, and her other siblings left home.

A year older than Mom, Dad had recently returned home from the army and was working for his father as a home builder in Chili, a suburb of Rochester on the city's west side. Dad came from a family of generous, industrious men and big-hearted, talented women. Dad's father, Bernie, and his uncle, Joe Entress, built so many homes in the Gates-Chili area and across Monroe County, New York that entire streets are named after them. For instance, we lived on Berna Lane, which intersected with Entress Drive, a street bearing our family's last name.

Unlike Mom, Dad was not a member of the St. Thomas Moore Club. His gregarious high school friend Bob Lombino invited him this once, to the Moore Club's picnic dinner. Little did Dad know that accepting this invitation would change his life.

As divine luck had it, Dad sat across the picnic table from Mom. Likely attending the event because steak was on the menu, Dad already devoured his food by the time Mom received her meal. She liked her meat well done, so hers required extra cooking. Mom then discovered she needed a knife before she could eat. Dad says he was happy to offer her his knife. It was a small but impactful gesture and an early sign of Dad's great willingness and capacity to provide later on.

"Dad, what did you and Mom talk about at dinner?" I recently asked him. "What kinds of questions did you ask Mom about herself?"

"She seemed very nice," he answered, but "I was the one fielding questions from all directions. I was the new guy there and everyone wanted to know where I live, where I went to school, and what church I went to." I am sure it didn't hurt that Dad was tall, dark, and handsome too. He may have been the most eligible bachelor in this group of young singles.

Mom remembers the car he came in. "He had a fancy car," she said. It was a 1964 Chevy Impala SS. The SS stood for "Super Sport." What an impression this automotive gem made on Mom, a city dweller who depended on the bus to get around. She needed a ride home that evening. Dad stepped up to the plate once again. He graciously drove miles out of his way to Mom's home near Kodak Park where her father, an immigrant from Ireland, worked many years as a pipefitter.

Enamored from day one, Dad asked Mom for her number and called within days to schedule an official date. They went bowling together and hit it off well. They began dating regularly, as Dad remembers:

> We went bowling or to a movie. Weekdays, I'd pick her up from work at the bank and take her out to dinner. On weekends, we enjoyed dinner at the Crescent Beach Hotel on the lake. They often had a live orchestra. I also took her to the Showboat on the water. On Sunday mornings we'd go to church together at Sacred Heart. On occasion, we ate breakfast with the Moore Club after church.

"He was the nicest guy I ever met," Mom always said about Dad. In addition, he was everything she was looking for in a man. Most importantly, Dad did not smoke or drink. Mom vowed she would never marry a drinker, not after witnessing first hand the violence, destruction, and death that came from her own father's addiction to alcohol.

Her entire family liked him too, even Mom's mother, Grandma Duggan, who could have held a grudge for what happened one night. It was the only mishap either remembers during the time they dated. Dad brought Mom home late one Friday evening, after her midnight curfew. They found the house locked up. They rang the doorbell and knocked, but nobody answered. Dad, always resourceful, created his own entrance. As he tells it:

I crawled through the milk box in the back of the house. It emptied me onto a small porch, but the inside door to the house was locked too. I crawled back outside. We went to the side door. It was a main door into the house. I broke the glass window, reached inside, and unlocked it, to let your mother in. I came back the next day with a sheet of glass and repaired that door. It looked brand new when I was done. We were probably thirty minutes past curfew that night. I bowled with St. Helen's on Friday nights, and we couldn't get on the lane until 9:30. There was a league before ours, and sometimes they ran late. I can't remember, but I may have wanted to stop for a hamburger afterwards. During Lent, we didn't eat meat on Fridays. I would order a late night hamburger and tell them to bring it out a minute after midnight.

I imagine Dad's handiwork with the window repair earned him points with Grandma Duggan, points that outweighed any penalty from the broken curfew. Mom, in fact, received a key to the house after this incident. As Judy observes, "Grandma Duggan thought very highly of Dad to not hold this against him."

Dad proposed to Mom three months after meeting her. At the young age of twenty-two, he knew what he was looking for in a wife and found it in Jean. "Dad, how did you know?" I asked him, wanting to learn from his experience. Here is what he said:

> I was back from the army and ready to settle down. I saw many abilities in your mother. She was a hard worker, and I knew should could cook and clean. She had faith, a good Catholic, practicing her religion. She was involved in the St. Thomas Moore Club. She went to Sacred Heart too and graduated from Nazareth Academy. I always asked myself, 'is this a person I can see myself spending the rest of my life with?' The answer was always "no" until I met her.

Had Mom been like most women, she would have jumped at Dad's proposal. Instead, she told him, "I'll think about it." Weighing on her heart and mind was the welfare of her own mother. She had been through much and was now sickly. Mom talked to a priest about the matter.

"Live your life," he encouraged her, giving her peace of mind to marry Dad. Still, Mom mulled the decision over until it occurred to her that she could not keep Dad waiting forever, or she may lose him. Weeks after the proposal, Mom gave Dad an answer.

"I'll marry you," she declared to him.

The following September they married at Sacred Heart Cathedral, the church Mom grew up in. They had a picture perfect reception for family and friends. It was a wedding Mom talked about for decades to come. "Do you want to see pictures?" Mom excitedly asked whenever the topic of their wedding came up. She would be halfway to the closet to pull out the albums, before we could even answer. She knew we loved looking at those pictures as much as she loved showing them off.

After they were married, Dad carried Mom into their new home, one he built for them during their nine-month engagement. It was a three-bedroom, 1,100 square foot ranch with a finished basement and a sturdy wooden deck off the back in the suburb of Chili on Douglas Drive.

During their early years of marriage, Dad earned a diploma from the Rochester Institute of Technology. He also worked at the University of Rochester, where he was quickly promoted and supervised construction projects. Mom, meanwhile, continued to work downtown at the bank. Their location on the bus line enabled her to continue taking the bus until she learned how to drive. She stopped working outside the home for a while when I, their eldest, was born.

Similar to every marriage, theirs had peaks and valleys. Mom recently told Grandma B that one of her biggest blessings is having three children who get along so well together, even though we are different in personality and interests. Dad said the same thing when I asked him to describe a highlight of their marriage. "Having you kids," he answered without hesitation.

"What about the lowest point, Dad?"

"When you were sick all those years," he replied.

"What about the last year, Dad, when Mom was going downhill? You were doing all of the cooking, cleaning, laundry, and shopping. This was on top of helping Mom with things she could no longer do for herself, such as putting on her socks and shoes? Wasn't that a low point?"

"Perhaps in looking back," he stated, "but not at the time." As Dad elaborates:

> It came on gradually. I didn't know we were heading toward a really low point. We were taking things day by day. I was doing more, but what I was doing didn't take me all day. We didn't do anything fancy. We were managing.

They managed so well that none of us realized how much assistance Mom actually needed, how burdened she was by the disease that was taking her life. Dad never complained during this time; nor did he ever boast about all he was doing. That is true love. It is the devotion God calls us to.

"Carry each other's burdens," He tells us, "...and in this way you will fulfill the law of Christ" (Galatians 6:2). The law of Christ is sacrificial love, loving God with all of our heart, soul, and mind, and loving our neighbors as ourselves (see Matthew 22:37-40).

***

At St. John's one afternoon, I asked Mom if she thinks I should get married. I recently broke an engagement to get married earlier in the year when some notable differences came to light. Before this, getting married was never a priority of mine. There was always so much else I wanted to do. But now, with the end of life more clearly in sight because of what was happening to Mom, these other priorities weighed on my mind as being potentially misplaced.

"What if I end up in a nursing home too?" I quietly pondered, "with no husband and no children? I'll be totally alone." Few if any friends visit regularly, definitely not every day, as we did for Mom.

"Get married only if you marry someone who is loving and faithful. That is what marriage is all about," Mom replied.

"Don't forget about Jesus. He will be with you, even if nobody else is not," said my friend Pam, when I later shared with her my growing concern about being unmarried. "And if you are neglected, you will die sooner and be with Him. Remember, '...to live is Christ and to die is gain'" (Philippians 1:21).

CHAPTER 8
Beautiful Character, Imperfect Love

CHAPTER EIGHT

Beautiful Character, Imperfect Love

Therefore we do not lose heart. Though outwardly we are wasting away, yet inwardly we are being renewed day by day.

2 CORINTHIANS 4:16

"What a beautiful time of year," I thought, as I made the drive into Rochester one afternoon in early October. Summerlike all week, it was nearly eighty degrees that day, and the foliage lining the I-490, which connects the City of Rochester to the New York State Thruway, was exceptionally pretty. The tree leaves formed a splattering of gorgeous jewel tones. "Autumn is much more beautiful than winter, spring, or summer," I concluded as I drove from my job in downtown Buffalo to St. John's to visit Mom.

In my eyes, Mom had grown incredibly beautiful too, not in color, as the leaves, but in character. "This disease is awful," she sometimes expressed to me.

I would always reply, "It is, but you are beautiful."

And I meant it. Isn't it true beauty that praises God with prayer and song every Sunday afternoon, even as one's voice fades to a whisper? Isn't it beautiful to find a heart of gratitude, someone who says thank you more than those abundantly blessed, even as they lose independence, relying on others to do what most of us take for granted? Confined to a wheelchair, true beauty finds genuine joy in watching others dance. It is broken hearted for those in need. True beauty is growing faith against a backdrop of loss and disappointing circumstances. This was Mom, the splendor of her character, the autumn of her soul, more fully revealed as her outer self wasted away and her physical abilities diminished.

Not a bone of self-pity existed in her body, even though she was the youngest one on her floor at St. John's. She was arguably the sickest one too. Never did I hear her yield to the temptation we all face daily. It is the enticement of unfavorably comparing our own situation to that of those around us, feeling we're been dealt a bad hand, compared to others we know who enjoy better health, more money, truer love, or happier lives.

Mom seemed to readily identify someone she considered worse off, such as those on her floor who could not talk or feed themselves. There was also the younger man we passed in the cafeteria with amputated legs. "Isn't that terrible? He looks young," she reflected. Mom felt badly for these individuals and fortunate for what she still had left.

Mom also thought much of her own mother, Helen Ruth Feeney Duggan, who lived years with a husband, Mom's Dad, who struggled with addiction and violent tendencies. He was in desperate need of help. If anyone inferred Mom had it bad, they were in for a story about Mom's mother who died at the age of fifty-five. "Every year past fifty-five, Mom considered a gift," remarks Judy.

Several friends and family members mentioned that Mom seems like a saint. This included Grandma B, who visited Mom shortly after she moved into St. John's. When I told Mom what some were saying about her, she replied, "I don't see myself as a saint. I'm just a follower of God."

I asked Mom if ALS has impacted her faith. She replied that it makes her feel closer to God. "I get a glimpse into how He suffered," she said. "I look at the cross on my wall more often." It was a crucifix that Dad brought in from home that hung on her wall in her bedroom at St. John's. It was a reminder of what Jesus endured. It was also a reminder of what He overcame, in being raised to life three days after His death on a cross.

"You know how much Jesus suffered," I replied, supposing more than Mom was saying. She immediately clarified and corrected me.

"I will never know what He went through. He suffered a lot more than me." This was Mom. She was a role model, friend, prayer warrior, sister in Christ, and one spiritually wise and humble. I loved her incredibly much. Yet, my love for her was imperfect. It was marred by own powerlessness over her disease and my continued fear of it.

***

One afternoon Mom said to me several times "this disease is awful; it's just awful. It's not nice to not be able to breathe." It broke my heart to see her in such distress. I prayed with her and told her the disease is terrible but she is beautiful, inside and out. I see her that way, and I know God does too. I also told her how I wish I could take some of her pain away. To this day, I am ashamed that I said "some" instead of "all."

Mom deserved better. Although I was powerless in my ability to take on any of my mother's pain, why couldn't I express unreserved willingness to do so? "What is wrong with you?" I later asked myself in complete disgust.

I actually considered saying "all" but before the word reached by lips, a word of warning shot through my head like a thunderbolt: "Be careful what you say; these words may come back to haunt you. Are you really ready to take on her disease?"

The answer is I was not, so, in a split second, I changed what was intended to be "all" to "some." I live with the regret. Yet, the incident offered a platform for the Lord to show us all, especially me, something about His perfect, all-powerful love, a love unhindered by the fear and vulnerability that impaired mine.

CHAPTER 9
Going Downhill, Called Upward

CHAPTER NINE

Going Downhill, Called Upward

I press on toward the goal to win the prize for which God has called me heavenward in Christ Jesus.

PHILIPPIANS 3:14

The time with Mom was passing quickly. "It's sad to see summer coming to an end," Mom said quietly as we turned the pages of the calendar on her wall. It was a good summer, with quality time together, visiting and taking advantage of some of the afternoon activities offered by St. John's.

Mom loved the summer concert series. Musicians from the community came in to play a variety of foot-stomping, hand-clapping music that residents were frequently familiar with. St. John's also has its own band. It was top notch. At times, we stopped by the auditorium to listen to them practice before dinner on Thursdays. As Mom and I regularly attended events and gatherings such as these, we came to know staff and others throughout the building.

Wherever Mom and I went, we invariably ran into someone we knew. They always greeted us with a big smile and hello. Lawrence, the chaplain in training, went even further. On a couple of occasions, he stopped what he was doing and offered to pray with us. These brief but impactful exchanges were good for Mom. They uplifted her spirits and reminded her that many care.

"Jean, you are always joyful," Chaplain Powell encouraged her one afternoon in later August. We ran into him downstairs on our way back from the cafeteria. That was another spot where we were warmly greeted by Jasmine, one of the workers in the cafeteria whom we came to know. Often there before any other patients, visitors, or staff arrived—usually 4:30 in the afternoon—we enjoyed our conversations with Jasmine, as I prepared a salad or ordered a veggie burger to take upstairs and eat with Mom.

"It must be hard to have your life interrupted midway through," a friend back home remarked, aware of the juggle between work in Buffalo and visits with Mom in Rochester several times a week. Most everything else, from volunteer commitments to any measure of a social life, came to an end.

September was a good reminder of the privilege of presence. Scrolling down Facebook's newsfeed after the long Labor Day weekend, I couldn't miss the many "first day" pictures friends with children proudly posted. Back to school is a milestone in every child, and every parent's life, sometimes exciting, sometimes scary. Either way, it is a great privilege to be there, walking with them through this passage of life.

I felt very similarly about time with Mom, as her body continued to decline and her soul prepared to pass into the hands of the Lord, the intersection of earth and Heaven. As an adult child, what a great privilege it is to be with one's parents during this time. Yet, it is not always easy.

***

Mom was in the worst shape I ever saw her in when I arrived Thursday afternoon, the second day of October. The curtain that divided her side of the room from Jane's and the common area they shared with the bathroom was closed when I arrived. This usually meant a nurse or doctor was tending to Mom. I dropped my bags near the door and waited. I wasn't troubled at all. Mom's various health needs brought nurses into her room regularly. Finally, the curtain swung open. "She is not doing so good this afternoon, but you can go in," announced her nurse.

I picked up my bags and headed immediately for Mom's bed, still not alarmed, until I saw my mother. She was awake, but she didn't immediately look at me, as she always did in the past, excited I was there and wanting to get out of bed. Mom was alert but her eyes looked glossy, and she was staring up towards the ceiling, as she lay in bed.

"Hi Mom," I said, holding back tears that came at the sight of her.

"I want to go up," she said.

"Up to where, Mom?" I asked her.

"To my room," she answered.

"Mom, you are in your room," I assured her. Nevertheless, she repeated this once or twice more, indicating to me that she wanted to go up to her room.

Although I didn't say anything more about it to Mom—it was taking all I had to stay composed for her—Mom's reference to her room couldn't help but remind me of what Jesus told his disciples about the eternal home He was preparing for them:

> Do not let your hearts be troubled. You believe in God; believe also in me. My Father's house has many rooms; if that were not so, would I have told you that I am going there to prepare a place for you? (John 14:1-2)

Was He giving her a glimpse of her eternal home? At the time, I did not let my mind go very far down that path. Rather, I unpacked my flute, assembled the three pieces of the instrument together, and played some of her favorites: *Amazing Grace*, *How Great Thou Art*, and *Oh Come Oh Come Emmanuel*. Gracious, even in her darkest hour, Mom clapped after each song I played.

Suddenly, the phone on Mom's nightstand rang. It was Dad, calling for me. "Your mother is being referred for hospice services," he said. St. John's telephoned him at home, just a short while after he returned home from his visit with her that day.

I wasn't shocked, not with the way Mom looked right now and the difficulty she had simply breathing and eating. For the first time since her diagnosis, she felt short of breath this week, just sitting calmly in her wheelchair.

Eating was a bit excruciating too. We sat on edge, eating with her, watching her closely, but trying not to be conspicuous. Mom often looked as if she was going to choke on her food. As the disease continued to wage war on the motor neuron cells controlling the muscles in my mother's esophagus, it would take seconds longer than normal for her food to go down after she chewed it. Every successful swallow seemed like a small miracle. Yet she asked that day to get up out of bed and go to the dining room. "She is doing this for you," her nurse said to me. "She'd be more comfortable in bed, but she is trying to be strong for you."

Before we went to dinner, where Mom ate mashed potatoes, Chaplain Shanley stopped by to talk with Mom and pray with us. "Do you think God is punishing you?" he asked her, as my blood pressure went up several notches after hearing the question. "Consider how Jesus suffered," he continued, as I sighed a breath of relief. "God could not love Him more."

Immediately after dinner, Mom asked to go back to bed. I told her I was staying the night with her. "Where are you going to sleep?" she asked, always a practical thinker. Her question reminded me of how Mom regularly asked me over the years if I was staying warm enough in my apartment. You would think I lived in a cabin without heat and electricity. But that was Mom. That her children had access to the basic necessities in life concerned her.

She also tended to be frequently cold. I remember staying over at their house one night, probably in town from Connecticut for a holiday. I remember Mom coming downstairs one evening to say goodnight to me before she headed up to bed. Underneath her pajamas she wore a turtleneck, and over them, she sported a thick, long robe, socks and slippers. It was a wonder to me she didn't melt!

"I am going to sleep in the recliner, Mom. I'll be right here if you need anything," I responded to her question at hand.

That night I prayed more than I slept. I also hummed for her, *How Great Thou Art* and *Amazing Grace*, two hymns that reflected the grace and greatness of God that we were about to witness.

CHAPTER 10
Home at Last

CHAPTER TEN

Home at Last

For I am convinced that neither death nor life, neither angels nor demons, neither the present nor the future, nor any powers, neither height nor depth, nor anything else in all creation, will be able to separate us from the love of God that is in Christ Jesus our Lord.

ROMANS 8:38-39

Mom awoke with the birds the next morning. Still in the chair at the foot of her bed, I sat up straight and leaned forward, so I could see her better. Sleeping at nearly a right angle to make her breathing easier, Mom could see me too.

"How are you feeling, Mom?" I asked her, as our eyes met.

"I'm alright," she replied.

"That's wonderful," I responded. "It looks like today is going to be a better day for you."

I was hoping for that and wanted to encourage Mom, but she did not look or seem all right. She could barely talk or hold a cup of thickened ice water up to her mouth. Later, she couldn't eat breakfast either and choked on the smallest spoonful of oatmeal. However, each time we would exchange glances that morning, she said to me, "I'm alright."

Dad arrived early that day, a couple hours before he usually came in. He knew I had stayed overnight and was planning to head back to Buffalo and go into work. However, I changed my mind. I e-mailed my boss from my phone, telling her I needed the day off. I did not want to leave.

As the day proceeded, my mother's doctor at St. John's told Dad and me how they were prepared to begin giving Mom morphine to help relieve pain, particularly from her shortness of breath. Her breathing was very labored, and all other options to lessen her symptoms had been exhausted.

The news crushed me. I have seen a couple of people over the course of my life on morphine. Both were very ill and near the end of their life. In my experience, which I know is limited, they lay in bed, until they die, mostly out of it, even if they can hear what is being said, as the doctor explained. Mom's doctor also assured me that there are people in the community who sometimes live on small doses of morphine to relieve pain. Yet I felt in my heart that any meaningful interaction with Mom would essentially cease.

"How much time does she have left?" I hesitantly asked her doctor.

"We don't know," she said. She added that a person could live up to two weeks after they stop eating. She also mentioned that how quickly death comes can sometimes depend on the level of peace one has with dying. Those who are not at harmony sometimes hang on to life longer.

"Mom knows where she is going. She isn't afraid to die. She has never been afraid of that," I confidently assured the doctor.

My heart nearly stopped beating every time the nurse came into Mom's room that day to ask her if she has any pain. They never asked once, but twice: "Jean, do you have any pain?"

"No," Mom answered, as I sighed a breath of relief.

"You don't have any pain anywhere?" they asked again.

"No," Mom answered. This scenario repeated itself about every two hours.

Was Mom masking what existed for our benefit? I felt certain she would have pointed to pain, had they asked her any other day that week. The other day she was uncomfortable, telling me how unpleasant having this disease is.

This remote possibility—that Mom acted strongly for our sake, saying she didn't have any pain when inside she was hurting—was ruled out when Mom didn't flinch a bit during a medical procedure later that day. It was one that causes a quick, but bearable shot of pain. "She didn't feel anything," her nurse assured me, sounding somewhat surprised herself.

With Mom alert and not in any discomfort, the day was a gift to all of us, including Judy and Mark who joined Dad and me later that afternoon. We sat with Mom; we comforted her; we brought her thickened ice water nearly every hour; and I played my flute a bit. A priest came in to pray with us too. We all held hands, praying the Lord's Prayer around Mom's bed. At the end of the prayer, I watched Mom do the sign of the cross. She also had communion, taking in her mouth the smallest piece of the host.

We witnessed her at a crossroads between this world and the next. "Don't worry about me," she said to me a couple of times, as I stood at her bedside. I do not know why she said that. It was almost as if God gave her a glimpse into what was ahead and she wanted to reassure me. She saw her room with Him ready; it was a place she wanted to go.

Her work and purpose on this earth were coming to an end. This is what her sister Pat truly believes. As we were sitting around Mom's bed that afternoon, the phone rang. It was my Aunt Pat. "How's your Mom doing?" she asked.

"We are all here, Aunt Pat, Dad, Judy, Mark, and myself. Mom had a really bad day yesterday."

"I want you to tell your mother that I believe in God because of her. I want her to know this."

"I will tell her, Aunt Pat. I know that will make her happy."

We all listened on as Mom repeatedly told her nurse and us that afternoon, "I want to give *it* up." It was a peculiar expression we never heard her use before, saying not that she wants to give up but indicating there is something within her, something about her, that she wanted to give up.

I did not ask Mom what she meant. I wish I could have, but deep down, I knew the end was drawing near. I could not let my mind or the conversation head in that direction without getting visibly upset. This would have troubled her and made her breathing even more difficult.

Later, however, all I could think about is how Jesus' death is described, "...he bowed his head and gave up his spirit" (John 19:30). When our body dies, our soul departs to be with God. What a beautiful, faithful, trusting soul He would receive in Mom.

That afternoon, one of Mom's nurses stopped in her room to say goodbye, telling Mom she was leaving a little early that day and will see her on Monday. Touched by the affection she showed toward Mom, I remember her telling Mom she loves her and giving her a hug and kiss.

What stands etched in Dad's memory is what Mom said to her nurse, "I'll be leaving too. My room is ready." Early the very next morning, on Saturday, October 4, 2014, exactly twenty weeks after her diagnosis, Mom's body died. Peacefully, while she was sleeping, her soul went up to be with the Lord. "Love you" are the last words she said to me. She left our family with a legacy of love and faith.

***

I shared the news of Mom's passing with Grandma B, who was praying for Mom. She was terribly saddened by the news. She was shocked too. "Your father told me on the phone last night she had two weeks left. I prayed God would take her sooner, so she wouldn't suffer." Grandma B said this was one of the few occasions in her life when God answered her prayer. Yet, later during our visit, she also wondered if God was angry with our family.

"Grandma, why do you think that?" I demanded of her.

"Because your mother died," she replied.

Grandma B outlived many of her friends and our close relatives, including one of her daughters, our aunt, who passed away a couple of years ago. She was only in her sixties. Grandma B wondered why God didn't take her instead. Why did He take such a good wife and mother, while Grandma B was blessed with years of life that most people do not experience?

> Grandma, we all die, one hundred percent of us. It has nothing to do with God being angry. Plus, Mom was ready; she loved the Lord with all of her mind, heart, and soul. I think about how elated Mom was to see Jesus in the world around her, to get a small glimpse into who He is while she lived on earth. What a precious gift it must be for her to see Him fully, face to face, in Heaven. This is the end she was living for.

After our visit, as I was leaving Grandma B's nursing home, a staff member at the front desk asked if Mom was in much pain before she died. She knew Mom from the many years Mom and Dad visited Grandma B together. I described to her how amazing it was that Mom was not in any pain the day before her death.

"I couldn't believe it," I confided in her.

"Jesus was her pain medication!" she exclaimed boldly and with great confidence.

It hit me at that very moment how our all-powerful, completely loving God stepped in and took away Mom's pain, maybe at the point where she could bear no more. It was the living manifestation of God's love, mercy, and power, as Mom was nearing the finish line of life, her frail body about ready to give out. Even this young woman from Grandma B's nursing home saw Him at work in our world.

I cannot help but think Mom did too, perhaps more clearly than she had ever seen Him before. As Dietrich Bonhoeffer describes in his book *The Cost of Discipleship*, if we reach a point where we fail to notice our own pain, it may be that we are looking so closely onto God and only God.[12]

Epilogue

And we know that in all things God works for the good of those who love him, who have been called according to his purpose.

ROMANS 8:28

Less than three months after God called Mom home, Grandma B passed away. It was just weeks before she would have turned ninety-seven. While no one can fully comprehend how our lives intertwine and how we affect one another, Mom may have played a part in pointing Grandma B more directly toward the ultimate maker and taker of life and the source of eternal life itself.

Before Mom died, Grandma B commonly mentioned how she was ready to die and be with Grandfather again. Understandably, Grandfather was the love of her life. They were married thirty-nine years, and he died in her arms, months before he planned to retire. He had been sick for some time.

"What about Jesus, Grandma B?" I would ask her. "Aren't you looking forward to seeing Him too?" Raised Catholic like Mom, Grandma B believed Jesus died on the cross for our sins. She knew that He rose from the dead, defeating the grave, and that through faith in Him, we too will have eternal life.

However, I wondered, "Why isn't she looking forward to seeing Him, the one she will spend eternity with in Heaven and the one who created Grandfather?"

"Oh, sure, Him too," she replied, matter-of-factly. However, the next time I visited, Grandma B mentioned he same thing about looking forward to being in Heaven with Grandfather.

Mom's death seemed to change her. Grandma B attended the funeral, and afterwards, I never heard her mention wanting to go to Heaven to be with Grandfather again. She told Judy, "I want to go to Heaven to be with God."

Some weeks later she told me quite spontaneously how she wished she took over organizing the annual family picnics since she could have used them as an opportunity to share her faith. Having never heard Grandma B talk like this or say anything of the kind, I was stunned by what she said. I was encouraged too, that she wanted to do this.

My heart's desire for Grandma B was for her to have the fervent, unshakable faith I saw in Mom. It was Mom's greatest desire too, for all those she loved. She knew Jesus, God in the flesh, fully human and fully God, was the source of her salvation. Jesus tells us all, "I am the way and the truth and the life. No one comes to the Father except through me" (John 14:6).

Jesus said this in response to his disciple Thomas who said he didn't know the way to Heaven (see John 14:5). Jesus' reply made it clear to Thomas and to all of us that the way is found through a person. It comes through a relationship with Jesus—knowing Him, having faith in Him, and following Him where He leads us for the time we are given in the world.

We don't have to be a member of a particular church, nor follow a Golden Rule or set of commandments, or even be what most consider a good person to get into Heaven. Consider the one thief on the cross next to Jesus who repented and expressed faith during his final hours of life:

> One of the criminals who hung there hurled insults at him: "Aren't you the Messiah? Save yourself and us!" But the other criminal rebuked him. "Don't you fear God," he said, "since you are under the same sentence? We are punished justly, for we are getting what our deeds deserve. But this man has done nothing wrong. Then he said, "Jesus, remember me when you come into your kingdom." Jesus answered him, "Truly I tell you, today you will be with me in paradise. (Luke 23:39-43)

Two thieves were there with Jesus; both were bad news, so wicked the authorities determined neither deserved to live. While both faced death, the one who turned from his wrongful ways and put his faith in Jesus was assured of being in Heaven that very day.

"Not fair!" some may say. "That stinking robber gets the same reward of Heaven as your mother and all of the saints on earth who lived their lives day in and day out trying to honor God?" He sure does. Salvation is a gift to all of us; it cannot be earned by anyone. If it could, then Jesus died on the cross for nothing. As God tells us:

> For it is by grace you have been saved, through faith—and this is not from yourselves, it is the gift of God—not by works, so that no one can boast. (Ephesians 2:8-9)

Yet, a relationship with Jesus is not only for when we die. It benefits us today, in the here and now. That is something the thief missed out on for most of his life. Sure, God promises us an eternal home that He prepares for all those who believe and follow Him.

He also promises us countless other things during our lifetime. He says, for instance, that His grace will be sufficient for us; that His power is perfected in our weaknesses (see 2 Corinthians 12:9-10). He tells us to be strong and courageous because He goes with us and will never leave us (see Deuteronomy 31:8). Do not worry, He says, but seek His Kingdom and all our needs will be provided for. He promises to work all things together for good (see Romans 8:28). As believers in God, our faith grows when we hear these truths and act on them.

Some may wonder if God is powerful and works everything for good, why didn't He miraculously heal Mom. Similar to Grandma B, they wonder why He let her die, when numerous people were praying for a miracle. I, for one, wanted more than anything to see her cured of ALS. But a cure in this life is not always how God responds. As Bo Stern writes in her book *Beautiful Battlefields*:

> Healing is a powerful sign to the world that God is real and strong and compassionate, and I am praying for healing every day. However, I don't believe it's the *only* way that God shows His goodness or demonstrates His love for us.

Bo tells how God's purposes involve bigger plans and a larger perspective that extend beyond our own lives. The saving of lives is what God cares much about. And He sometimes uses rotten circumstances in our lives to bring eternal blessings to others. Take Joseph from the Old Testament as an example.

Joseph was the great grandson of Abraham. Abraham is described in the Bible as the father of all those who believe in God. Abraham is often remembered for how he and his wife Sarah had their first child, Isaac, when Abraham was one hundred years old and Sarah was ninety. Joseph endured years of suffering. He was sold into slavery by his brothers, then falsely accused by his employer. He even served time in prison for an offense he did not commit.

Yet God used all of these offenses against Joseph to ultimately reposition him and raise him up. After years of being a slave, then a prisoner, Joseph became second in command of Egypt. In this position of authority, Joseph saved the lives of his family—the people of Israel—during years of a grave famine. What others meant for evil, God used for good. It was bountiful good that came from Joseph's rotten circumstances. Through it all, Joseph never lost faith in God, who is present in our battles, blessings and the ordinary of life.

We must trust that God knows what is best from a much larger, eternal perspective than human beings are capable of, being bound by space and time. Might this be the case in our family? Judy is convinced.

> He allowed Mom to get a disease with no cure and no treatment, where we had to accept death, something Mom was ready for. What if she got cancer and then didn't get treatment? We would have been furious. We would have accused her of giving up. Look at how we acted before she was diagnosed, when we thought she needed a knee replacement, and didn't get one. She would not have been the same person in our eyes as she is today, if it happened any other way. Now we see Mom as she saw her mother, as a saint. With death certain and a healthy life not an option, we clearly see her faith, her true love of God.

We also got to know God Himself better. It is one thing to read in the Bible how God provided for Joseph and all of the other saints who have gone before us during the valleys of their lives. It is another thing to experience His love and provision in our own lives and to see His power in our circumstances.

That was Jesus' prayer—not that we have a carefree and forever healthy life—but that we know the one true God and Jesus Christ whom God sent into the world, since this is eternal life (see John 17:3). Back at Strong Memorial Hospital in May, Mom was eager to share with us how she saw a cross in her window. For her, that cross was an encouraging and powerful reminder of Jesus and what He endured to make a way to Heaven for her and for all who put their faith in Him.

Letters from Mom

Let love and faithfulness never leave you; bind them around your neck, write them on the tablet of your heart.

PROVERBS 3:3

Here I share with you a small sampling of the e-mails and letters I received from Mom over the years. She began writing to me when I moved away from home to the Hartford, Connecticut area. I took a job as an actuarial analyst at Cigna Corporation, after graduating from the University of Rochester. Occasionally she would send me small gifts with her letters: hand-knitted slippers, homemade molasses cookies, small necklaces, news clippings from the local paper, and pocket-sized booklets from the Salesian Missions offering poems and inspirational stories. Even when I moved back to New York, closer to home and able to visit more often, Mom continued writing.

Invariably she wrote these notes on behalf of her and Dad, always signing them "Love, Mom and Dad." Sometimes she addressed them to me as simply "Ana." She knew I liked that middle name but I've changed all of those salutations to include my first name Sharon, to avoid any confusion by you, my readers.

My email account shows nearly 800 emails from her and Dad between November 2006, when I created that account, and when Mom was diagnosed with ALS and no longer home and able to e-mail any longer. That is roughly one or two notes a week. This is in addition to a large stack of hand-written letters I have from her from over the years.

It is difficult to fully describe why I saved them all. Like Mom, I tend to be a minimalist. Quite regularly, I donate clothes, books, CDs, and other items I no longer use to various causes and second hand shops in town. I think it was simply my love for her and her sincere heart that marked them in my mind, and in my closet, as too special to discard.

God tells us in the Bible that what we communicate to others is a reflection of what is in our heart (see Luke 6:45 and Matthew 12:34). I share these letters and emails with you, so you can better know my mother, her character, and her heart. I hope they shed light on her gentle, unassuming nature, her incredibly thankful attitude, her consistency and encouraging manner and words, and her faith in God and ability to see Him in the world around her.

June 18, 2013

Hi Sharon Ana,

We were happy to see you on Fathers Day. We wish to thank you for the cinnamon bread and the delicious molasses cookies that you brought to us. Also thanks for all your help on Sunday such as washing the dishes. Also thanks for the delicious salad you brought. We are using it up this week. We appreciate all you did for us to make our job easier. The bouquet of flowers looks so nice on our table. We are enjoying them so much. May God bless on the nice things you do for others.

Have a good week, Sharon.

Love,

Mom and Dad

April 9, 2012

Hi Sharon Ana,

We wish to tell you that we were very happy that you could come and spend Easter with us. Also we are happy you had a good drive home too. We wish to thank you for the delicious berry pie you made for us. We had it for supper tonight and we have enough for tomorrow night too. It was so nice of you to bake it for us. Also thanks for the bouquet of flowers. They are beautiful and are displayed on our dining room table. Also thanks for the lovely Easter card too and the lovely message on it too. We love your company and it is remarkable about the gift you have about the knowledge of God, We love to hear your knowledge about different things too. We have been blessed by God to have you as our beautiful daughter. I look forward to talking to you soon.

Have a good week, Sharon.

Love,

Mom and Dad

January 10, 2012

Hi Sharon,

Thanks for the message. I thought you might like to read about the football player, Tim Tebow. He is a good example for the other players. And you are a good example for other people who are looking for God but do not know about Him. You know a lot about God and you are gifted in your religion and can pass it on to others. We hope and pray for your trip that everything works out well for you. We will look forward for you to let us know all about the trip. Also we wish to thank you for the beautiful flowers that you gave us. They look beautiful on our table. And we think of you whenever we see them. If you need our help with anything, please let us know.

Love,

Mom and Dad

January 7, 2012

Hi Sharon Ana,

It was nice to hear from you. I am happy you liked the message from the pope. It is a grace from God if He gives a sickness or a cross to bear. It means He wants you to be in heaven with Him. Also we are happy you can come and have supper with us. We look forward to you coming and also want to let you know you do not have to bring the dessert or salad because we have the dessert and the salad here, but thanks for the offer. Have a good safe trip. Also Dad wants you to park in the driveway as he will park at the clubhouse.

Have a good week, Sharon.

Love,

Mom and Dad

September 20, 2011

Hello Sharon Ana,

It was so nice to hear from you. The Bible has eight beatitudes and it is under Matthew 5. Blessed is the clean of heart, for they shall see God. Thanks for the nice remark but we think you know much about God too. You bring so much happiness to others. I am sure God is very happy with all you do for him.

Have a nice week, Sharon.

Love,

Mom and Dad

April 9, 2011

Hi Sharon Ana,

It was nice to hear from you. I am happy you enjoyed the story about St. Terese. St. Terese wrote a book called The Story of a Soul. St. Terese joined the convent went she was 15 yrs. old. St. Terese of Lisieux said I am a very little soul and can offer very little things to our Lord. I am looking forward to your call tomorrow evening.

Love,

Mom and Dad

March 17, 2011

Hi Sharon,

We are happy you enjoyed the card. Also thanks for your lovely St. Patrick's card too. We received it today and it was so thoughtful of you. It was a lovely day today for St. Patrick's Day. St. Patrick came from England and went to Ireland to convert the people to Christianity. We look forward to talking to you soon. Have a nice week, Sharon.

Love,

Mom and Dad

February 4, 2011

Hi Sharon Ana,

I thought you might like to read this News Story about Christ's resurrection is Victory Over Sickness, Pope Says.

Love,

Mom and Dad

July 11, 2010

Hi Sharon Ana,

We had a nice drive home and got home at 7:10 pm. We were so happy we came to see you and visit with you. And we would like to thank you for the lovely dinner you gave to us. The pizza was delicious the fruit salad was delicious and the lemon pie shell was delicious too. We were so happy to see the beautiful birds on your porch. God must send them to you. Also you have a beautiful knowledge of God and can speak so elegantly about Him. God must be so happy with your knowledge of Him. We had a lovely time but the time did go by so quickly. We hope you have a good week and say hello to Biden for us. Also thanks for all the food you gave to us. We will truly enjoy it.

Love,

Mom and Dad

February 15, 2010

Hi Sharon Ana,

I thought you might like to read this story The Church Recognizes the Face of Jesus in the Poor. Sharon Ana, you have the Love of Jesus in you amid the trials you are going through. We all go through trials but knowing God helps us go through them.

Love,

Mom and Dad

October 7, 2009

Hi Sharon Ana,

Thanks for the message. The movers did a good job moving us. It took the one hour and half to move us and then one hour to move us here. We have almost everything put away. We are adjusting well to the move. The furniture is all in place too. We got the washer and dryer in action too. Dad had to get the maintenance to put a new plug and three prong on the dryer. They came today while we were at Wegmans for dinner and for a few items. Guess what, on Tuesday, one of the movers put our bed in the apt. He told us that there was a rose on the headboard and that was normal for old wood from many years ago. So I looked at the headboard and it looks like Jesus is on the headboard. Dad saw it and believes it too. That bedroom outfit was given to us from Grandma and Grandpa when we were just married. Dad said the wood is about 80 years old. So God is with us wherever we go....

Have a nice week, Sharon.

Love,

Mom and Dad

September 19, 2009

Hi Sharon Ana,

We would like to thank you so much for the lovely Anniversary card you gave to us. Also thanks so much for sending A Special Dinner Gift certificate For You. Thanks for the lovely message on the certificate. Also the pictures you put on the certificate bring back many memories from 44 yrs ago. Sharon Ana, you did a beautiful job in making the certificate so special which we will always treasure. God has been good to us with a nice long marriage which we are very grateful for and He gave us three beautiful children too which we are very grateful for. I look forward to talking to you soon.

Have a nice week, Sharon.

Love,

Mom and Dad

February 8, 2009

Hi Sharon,

We got home about 7:30 pm. we had a nice drive home and the weather was perfect. The traffic was heavy. We had a nice time visiting with you. Also thanks for treating us to that nice supper with we had with you. We feel bad that Biden did not come out of the bedroom to visit with us. Maybe the next time we visit you, she will come out of the bedroom. We wish you good luck when you meet with the Crisis Center. Hope and pray it will work out well for you. You will have to let us know about it. It was so nice of you to give a donation to Fr. Groesche and Mother Angelica. It will make them so happy and know God will be so happy too. God loves you more than you can imagine. Sharon, have a good week and enjoy this nice weather. It was so nice of you to make us banana bread. I know we will enjoy it.

I will talk to you soon, Sharon

Have a nice week, Sharon

Love,

Mom and Dad

February 7, 2009

Hi Sharon,

I will bring the information to you about the website of Jesus Christ and the videos of His life that I listen to. We look forward to seeing you soon.

Love,

Mom and Dad

June 17, 2007

Hi Sharon,

We are happy you had a nice drive home. We are happy you could come and help us celebrate Dad's Father Day and Mark's birthday. Dad was happy with all his cards and lovely gifts especially the bag that was made with screws and nails. He enjoyed all the work you did on that bag. You are very artistic, Sharon.

Thanks for the horderves. The fruit was delicious and we all enjoy it so much with the strawberries, watermelon and grapes and cheddar mix were very good. Also thanks for the pie and kuchen too. It was so nice of you to think of us so much. We look forward to seeing you on Wednesday. It was nice you saw a rainbow going home. God is very majestic today to let people know He is around.

Dad is so happy that he received a subscription for Consumers Report and wants to thank you so much for it.

Have a good week, Sharon

Love,

Mom and Dad

June 21, 2000

Dear Sharon,

Thank you so much for the lovely orchid plant for Mother's Dad. It was so nice of you. Also Dad thanks you for the nuts too for Father's Day. He will enjoy them too. We hope and pray everything will work out for you. I went to St. Pius Church today and the pastor says when you do what God wants you to do, then you will be happy even when other people object to what you do. Father Foster Rogers is a wonderful priest and gives good sermons and is well liked. He sends everyone in the parish birthday cards. Sharon, we would like to visit you sometime. You can let us know when you're free. Have a good week and we will keep you in our prayers.

Love,

Mom and Dad

p.s. June 21 is your Grandfather's birthday, Sharon

June 3, 1998

Hi Sharon,

How are you doing? Do you like working at your job? We are doing good. We are getting together for Mark's birthday party. We are planning on having spaghetti for dinner and making him a cake.

Grandma and Judy are coming over and we hope you can come also, Sharon. We would be so happy to see you.

We took pictures of Mark on Saturday before he went to the Senior Ball with Teresa. He looked so handsome in his tuxedo and it fitted him perfectly. It looked like it was made for Mark.

The Town of Chili is offering lessons on how to use the computer in the library and I am signed up for them. The first one starts June 18 and also on June 30.

Well Sharon, we will keep you in our prayers and hope everything works out well for you. Sharon, I always wear a medal of our Lord or keep it in my pocket and He always keeps me safe and I know that I can trust him always.

Love,

Mom and Dad

This last letter, penned nearly twenty years ago, caught my attention. I believe it sheds great light on a miniature card that came from Mom. I found this tiny card tucked inside another letter from her. On the front was a picture of a rainbow and cross. There was also a poem about the cross of Christ and what it must have meant to my mother. Perhaps she picked up this card at church, or maybe it came to her in the mail. I do not know. A Google search of the poem pointed to Vera Mae Thomas as the author.

She describes carrying a cross in her pocket, as a reminder that she belongs to the Lord wherever she may be. She knows that cross is not a lucky charm, nor will it protect her from everything in life that could harm her or go wrong. Rather, it represents an understanding between her and her Savior who died on that cross but did not stay dead. It reminds her to be thankful each day for the many blessings, and to strive to live for Him in all she does and says. It is a reminder, too, of peace and comfort that are hers to have, knowing she is in His loving hands and care.

On the back of the card are verses from the Bible, ones to consider for those who want Heaven to be their eternal home. They include:

> For God so loved the world that he gave his one and only Son, that whoever believes in him shall not perish but have eternal life. (John 3:16)

> ...for all have sinned and fall short of the glory of God... (Romans 3:23)

> Jesus answered, "I am the way and the truth and the life. No one comes to the Father except through me. (John 14:6)

> Believe in the Lord Jesus, and you will be saved... (Acts 16:31)

Where are you in your journey of faith? Have you ever asked Jesus to be your personal Savior? If you have not, you can do this now, right from where you are. The card my mother gave me presents a prayer that you could offer to God to invite him into your life. It goes something like this:

> Dear Lord Jesus, I believe that You are God in the flesh. I believe that You died on the cross for my sins. It is where Your love poured out for me and for all of humanity. I believe that You rose from the dead, defeating death and the cross. Lord, I turn from doing things my own way. I repent of things I do, say, and think about that do not honor You and Your will for my life. I ask for Your forgiveness and mercy. I invite You into my life, and I thank You for the gift of eternal life. I place my trust in You and will strive each day to live for You, as you reveal Yourself to me in your word to us in the Bible. Thank you for Your

love, your mercy, and for the gift of eternity with You.

It is my prayer for all of those reading this book that the reality of God's presence and love grow in your heart and bring you peace, courage, and joy all of the days of your life. No matter what you or a loved one may be going through, or where you find yourself on your journey of faith, I pray you know that your life has purpose and can be a tremendous blessing to those around you until the time our Heavenly Father calls you home. God bless you, dear readers, and thank you very much for the time you spent with this book.

Resources

*Therefore encourage one another and
build each other up....*

1 Thessalonians 5:11

ALS Association, http://www.alsa.org. Find information on ALS, local chapter locations, resources, latest research, and ways to get involved.

Zondervan, Publishing H. *Niv Study Bible: New International Version.* S.l.: Zondervan, 2011. Print. This is wonderful Bible to get for yourself or to give as a gift.

Stern, Bo. *Beautiful Battlefields.* Colorado Springs, CO: NavPress, 2013. Print. Bo's husband lived with ALS, and this family simply amazed me with their faith, strength, and joy.

Tada, Joni E. *Joni: An Unforgettable Story.* Grand Rapids, Mich: Zondervan, 2001. Print. A diving accident left Joni paralyzed and wheelchair bound. This is a powerful story of tragedy and triumph.

The Chapel, and Jerry Gillis. "Bad Things, God's People." 8 Jul. 2007, available online in audio or video format at https://thechapel.com/sermons/2007-messages/bad-things--gods-people/
I listened to this message and others in my car, as I commuted back and forth to visit my mother. These messages kept me

grounded in God's word and strong in faith. They are available online. They can be also ordered on CD and DVD from the Chapel. See the Chapel's website for contact information.

The Chapel, and Jerry Gillis. Gillis. "The Mystery of Tragedy." 22 Feb. 2009, available online in audio or video format at http://thechapel.com/sermons/2009-messages/the-mystery-of-tragedy/

The Chapel, and Jerry Gillis. "A Prayer Of Death And Life." The Chapel. 14 Apr. 2014, available online in audio and video format at https://thechapel.com/sermons/fly-on-the-wall/a-prayer-of-death-and-life/

Vujicic, Nick. *Life Without Limits: Inspiration for a Ridiculously Good Life*. New York: Doubleday, 2010. Print. Nick was born without arms and legs, yet he lives life abundantly. With God, all things are possible. Nick is living proof. Whatever your abilities or limitations, you will be inspired by his story.

Notes

Do not withhold good from those to whom it is due, when it is in your power to act.

PROVERBS 3:27

---

[1] "Biography." The Official Website of Lou Gehrig. N.p., n.d. Web. 08 Oct. 2016.

[2] The ALS Association. "Facts You Should Know." ALSA.org. N.p., n.d. Web. 08 Oct. 2016. Steven Hawkings is an example of one with ALS who has beaten the odds, in terms of life expectancy, and exceeded all expectations. Hawkings was diagnosed with ALS at the age of 21. Today, he is 74. For more information, see Harmon, Katherine, "How Has Stephen Hawking Lived Past 70 with ALS?" Scientific American. N.p., 07 Jan. 2012. Web. 08 Oct. 2016.

[3] "Amyotrophic Lateral Sclerosis." Symptoms and Causes. Mayo Clinic, n.d. Web. 08 Oct. 2016.

[4] Id.

[5] "This Time Voters Will Decide On 'Right-To-Die' Law In Colorado." CBS Denver. 24 Sept. 2016. Web. 08 Oct. 2016.

[6] Tribune News Services. "California Woman with ALS Holds Party for Friends, Family before Ending Her Life." Chicago Tribune, 11 Aug. 2016. Web. 08 Oct. 2016.

[7] Payton, Laura. "Supreme Court Says Yes to Doctor-assisted Suicide in Specific Cases." CBC News. 06 Feb. 2015. Web. 08 Oct. 2016.

[8] University of Rochester Medical Center. "Amyotrophic Lateral Sclerosis (ALS) Clinic - Clinical Services - Neurology - University of Rochester Medical Center." Amyotrophic Lateral Sclerosis (ALS) Clinic - Clinical Services - Neurology - University of Rochester Medical Center. N.p., n.d. Web. 08 Oct. 2016.

[9] "Find and Compare Nursing Homes | Nursing Home Compare." Find and Compare Nursing Homes | Nursing Home Compare. U.S. Centers for Medicare and Medicaid Services, n.d. Web. 08 Oct. 2016.

[10] "St. John's History - St. John's, Rochester, NY." St. John's, n.d. Web. 08 Oct. 2016.

[11] Powell, Darryl. "Why We Are Called St. John's - St. John's, Rochester, NY." St. John's, Rochester, NY. N.p., 7 Apr. 2015. Web. 08 Oct. 2016.

[12] Bonhoeffer, Dietrich. The Cost of Discipleship." New York: Simon & Schuster, 1959. Print. See page 88 for Dietrich's exact words on this subject.

Made in the USA
Lexington, KY
29 April 2017